P · O · C · K · E · T · S

INSECTS

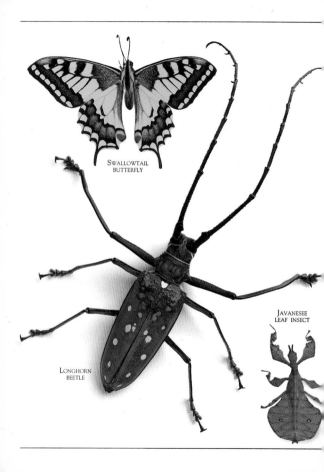

SWALLOWTAIL
BUTTERFLY

JAVANESEE
LEAF INSECT

LONGHORN
BEETLE

P · O · C · K · E · T · S

INSECTS

Written by
LAURENCE MOUND
and STEPHEN BROOKS

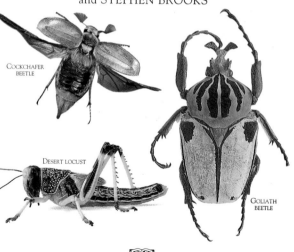

COCKCHAFER
BEETLE

DESERT LOCUST

GOLIATH
BEETLE

A DORLING KINDERSLEY BOOK

Editor Bernadette Crowley
Art editor Ann Cannings
Senior editor Susan McKeever
Senior art editor Helen Senior
Picture research Caroline Brooke
Production Louise Barratt
US editor Jill Hamilton
US consultant Eric Quinter, Department of
Entomology, American
Museum of Natural History

First American Edition, 1995
8 10 9

Published in the United States by DK Publishing, Inc.
95 Madison Avenue, New York, New York 10016

Visit us on the World Wide Web at http://www.dk.com

Library of Congress Cataloging-in-Publication Data
Mound, L.A. (Laurence Alfred)
Insects / by Laurence Mound & Stephen Brooks – 1st American ed.
p cm. – (A DK pocket)
Includes index.
ISBN 1-56458-887-4
1. Insects - Juvenile literature. [1. Insects.] I. Brooks, S.J. II. Title. III. Series.
QL467.2.M683 1995
595.7 – dc20   94-31842
                                                CIP
                                                AC
Color reproduction by Colourscan, Singapore
Printed and bound in Italy by L.E.G.O.

CONTENTS

How to use this book 8

INTRODUCTION TO INSECTS 10

What is an insect? 12
The first insects 14
Types of insect 16
Metamorphosis 22
How insects move 26
Insect senses 32
How insects feed 36
Courtship, birth, and growth 40
Insect societies 48
Hunting and hiding 52
Where insects live 60

TEMPERATE WOODLAND 62

About the habitat 64
Oak tree 66

Tree canopy 68
Woodland butterflies 70
Treetrunks and branches 72
Ground level 74

GRASSLANDS AND HEATHLANDS 76

About the habitat 78
Grassland insects 80
Heathland insects 82

LAKES AND RIVERS 84

About the habitat 86
Water surface insects 88
Underwater insects 90

TROPICAL FOREST 92

About the habitat 94
In the canopy 96
Nests in the canopy 98
Brilliant butterflies 100
Tropical butterflies 102
Horned beetles 104
The largest insects 106
Stick and leaf insects 108
Armies on the ground 110

DESERTS, CAVES, AND SOIL 112

About the habitat 114
Desert insects 116
Cave insects 118
Soil insects 120

TOWNS AND GARDENS 122

About the habitat 124
Household insects 126
Garden insects 128
Friends and foes 130
Bees and pollination 132

REFERENCE SECTION 134

Insect classification 136
Studying insects 140
Projects at home 142
Endangered habitats 144
Insect records 146

Resources 148
Glossary 150
Index 154

HOW TO USE THIS BOOK

These pages show you how to use *Pockets: Insects*. The book is divided into several sections. The main section consists of information on insects from different habitats. There is also an introductory section at the front, and a reference section at the back. Each new section begins with a picture page.

HABITATS

The insects are arranged into habitats. In each habitat section you will find information on the habitat, and examples of the types of insects that live there and how they adapt to their environment.

Running head   *Label*

Corner coding

Heading

ABOUT THE HABITAT

TEMPERATE WOODLANDS are often dominated by one tree species, such as oak, which is deciduous (the trees lose their leaves in winter). The types of insect found, and their numbers, will vary with the seasons, as well as with the types of tree species in the woodlands.

Introduction

DRAINING
Forests in wetlands have many different plant species. But people often drain this habitat because it is good for farming. Draining kills plants such as milk-parsley, the only plant the English swallowtail butterfly will breed on. This beautiful insect is now rarely seen.

Although the English swallowtail will lay eggs only on milk-parsley, adults eat a variety of flowers.

Size indicator

CORNER CODING
Corners of the pages are color coded to remind you which habitat section you are in.

- ■ TEMPERATE WOODLAND
- ■ GRASSLANDS AND HEATHLANDS
- ■ LAKES AND RIVERS
- ■ TROPICAL FOREST
- ■ DESERTS, CAVES, AND SOIL
- ■ TOWNS AND GARDENS

HEADING
This describes the subject of the page. This page is about the temperate woodland habitat. If a subject continues over several pages, the same heading applies.

INTRODUCTION
This provides a clear, general overview of the subject. After reading this, you should have an idea what the pages are about.

CAPTIONS
AND ANNOTATIONS
Each illustration has a caption. Annotations, in *italics*, point out features of an illustration and usually have leader lines.

RUNNING HEADS

...ese remind you which
...tion you are in. The left-
...nd page gives the section
...me. The right-hand page
...es the subject. This
...e, About the Habitat,
... the Temperate
...odland section.

FACT BOXES

Many pages have fact
boxes. These contain
at-a-glance information
about the subject. This
fact box gives details
such as how many
insect species live
in oak trees.

Fact box   Annotation

ABOUT THE HABITAT

...CTS
...of sole
...itent
...iety. Blue
... that live on
...at 5,000
...

...ver 280
... can live
...

...ainforests
...are
... faster than
...rests.

Bumblebees are
very common in
woodland.

FLOWERS
Woodlands contain
many types of flower.
These attract various species
of insect, such as bumblebees,
which nest in the ground in
animal burrows and pollinate
many woodland flowers.

VAPORER MOTH CATERPILLAR
This attractive caterpillar eats the
leaves of many different trees in
Europe and North America.
It will also attack
rosebushes and
heather plants.

Vaporer moth
caterpillar is covered
with tufts of hair.

PROCESSIONS
Conifer forests have
fewer types of plant and
animal than deciduous
forests, although some, such as
processionary moth caterpillars, can be
common. These are named for their habit
of following each other head to tail.

6 5

Caption

SIZE INDICATORS

Some insect pictures have
a magnifying glass with a
plus (+) or minus (–) sign
and a number. This shows
how much bigger (+)
or smaller (–)
the picture is
from life size.

REFERENCE SECTION

INSECT CLASSIFICATION

...out million or so named insect species are part of
... animal kingdom, which includes every other
...mal species. In order to discuss the different species,
...classify them into a series of categories according
...the features they have in common. The largest
...egory is the kingdom, which includes all animals.
The kingdom is divided into
smaller categories, which
are further divided until the
species level
is reached.

KINGDOM
Animal

PHYLUM
Arthropoda - animals with
jointed legs

CLASS
Insecta - three air orifice
species, arranged into 32 orders

ORDER
Hymenoptera - includes ants,
bees, and wasps.

FAMILY
Apidae - includes 5,700
species of bees.

GENUS
Formica - Latin for ant. The
genus contains 155 species

SPECIES
Formica rufa - Latin for red ant.

Living things can breed only
with members of their own
species. For example, a honeybee
cannot breed with another species. Some aploid
species rarely breed since they produce
offspring without mating, and most ants in a
nest are sterile workers that cannot breed.

1 1 4

CLASS	SPECIES	CHARACTERISTICS
COLLEMBOLA	*Springtails*	Primitive wingless insects, often found on soil or wet countries; incomplete metamorphosis
THYSANURA	*Silverfish*	Primitive wingless insects, found in caves and damp houses; incomplete metamorphosis
EPHEMEROPTERA	*Mayflies*	Larvae found in freshwater, adults have no feeding apparatus and live only a few days; incomplete metamorphosis
ODONATA	Dragonflies and damselflies	Generally large insects, found in freshwater, carnivorous or herbivorous; larvae are predators on freshwater; incomplete metamorphosis
PLECOPTERA	*Stoneflies*	Adults are either herbivorous or do not feed at all and usually live along riverbanks; larvae live in freshwater; incomplete metamorphosis
BLATTODEA	*Cockroaches*	Omnivorous (eating both animals and plants) insects, often scavengers, found worldwide; incomplete metamorphosis
ISOPTERA	Termites, also known as white ants	Social insects that live in vast colonies, each with one queen who lays all the eggs, some species feed on wood; incomplete metamorphosis
MANTODEA	*Mantids*	Predatory insects with large eyes and grasping front legs, found mostly in the tropics; incomplete metamorphosis

1 1 7

The reference section pages are yellow
and appear at the back of the book.
On these, you will find useful facts,
figures, and charts. These pages show
the classification of insects and how
they fit into the animal kingdom

INDEX

Their are two indexes at the back of the
book – a subject index and a latin name
index. The subject index lists every subject
alphabetically. The latin name index lists
the latin name of all the insects in the book.

...BELS

...r extra clarity, some pictures
...e accompanied by labels. These
...ay provide extra information,
... identify a picture when it is
...t immediately obvious what
...is from the text.

INTRODUCTION TO INSECTS

WHAT IS AN INSECT? 12

THE FIRST INSECTS 14

TYPES OF INSECT 16

METAMORPHOSIS 22

HOW INSECTS MOVE 26

INSECT SENSES 32

HOW INSECTS FEED 36

COURTSHIP, BIRTH, AND GROWTH 40

NESTS AND SOCIETIES 48

HUNTING AND HIDING 52

WHERE INSECTS LIVE 60

WHAT IS AN INSECT?

THERE ARE AT LEAST one million named insect speci
– they are the most abundant animals on earth. All
insects have six legs, and their skeleton is on the
outside of their body. This outer
skeleton forms a hard,
protective armor around
the soft internal organs.

*The antennae
of insects can
sense smells
and vibrations
in the air.*

DISSECTED
BEETLE

Eye

*First part of
thorax bears
the front legs.*

*Jointed
front leg*

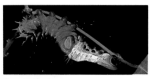

SHEDDING SKIN

An immature insect is called a nymph.
As each nymph feeds and grows, it must
shed its hard outer skin, which is also
called an exoskeleton. When it grows
too big for its skin, the skin splits,
revealing a new, larger skin underneath.

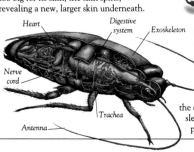

Heart   *Digestive
system*   *Exoskeleton*

*Nerve
cord*

Trachea

Antenna

INTERNAL ANATOMY

A typical insect breathes
through holes in its sides
distributes air around
body in tubes callec
tracheae. It has a r
cord which runs bene
the digestive system. The heart,
slender tube with several holes
pumps blood around the bod

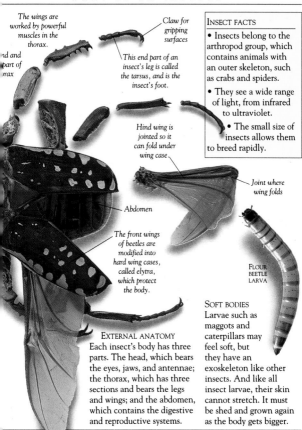

The wings are worked by powerful muscles in the thorax.

...nd and ...art of ...orax

Claw for gripping surfaces

This end part of an insect's leg is called the tarsus, and is the insect's foot.

Hind wing is jointed so it can fold under wing case

Joint where wing folds

Abdomen

The front wings of beetles are modified into hard wing cases, called elytra, which protect the body.

FLOUR BEETLE LARVA

INSECT FACTS

• Insects belong to the arthropod group, which contains animals with an outer skeleton, such as crabs and spiders.

• They see a wide range of light, from infrared to ultraviolet.

• The small size of insects allows them to breed rapidly.

EXTERNAL ANATOMY
Each insect's body has three parts. The head, which bears the eyes, jaws, and antennae; the thorax, which has three sections and bears the legs and wings; and the abdomen, which contains the digestive and reproductive systems.

SOFT BODIES
Larvae such as maggots and caterpillars may feel soft, but they have an exoskeleton like other insects. And like all insect larvae, their skin cannot stretch. It must be shed and grown again as the body gets bigger.

1 3

THE FIRST INSECTS

INSECTS WERE the first animals to fly. They appeared 300 million years ago – long before humans, and even before the dinosaurs. The ancient insect species are now extinct, but some were similar to modern dragonflies and cockroaches.

INSECT IN AMBER
Amber is the fossilized tree resin which came from pine trees over 40 million years ago. Well-preserved ancient insects are sometimes found in amber. This bee is in copal, which is similar to amber but not as old.

FLOWER FOOD
When flowering plants evolved 100 million years ago, insects gained two important new foods – pollen and nectar. Insec thrived on these foods. They pollinated the flowers, and many new species of plants and insects evolved togethe

FIRST INSECT FACTS

• The oldest known fossil insect is a springtail that lived 400 million years ago.

• Some of the earliest insects seem to have had three pairs of wings.

• The oldest known butterfly or moth is known from England 190 million years ago.

MODERN
EARWIG

ROCK REMAINS
This fossil of an earwig was found in 35-million-year-old lake sediment in Colorado. The fossil shows how similar in shape ancient earwigs were to modern ones.

Fossil earwig

FOSSIL DRAGONFLY
Dragonflies were one of the first types of
insect. Fossils show that they have not
changed very much in appearance
over millions of years. Some
ancient dragonflies were very
large and may have had wing-
spans of over 2 ft (60 cm).
This dragonfly fossil,
found in southern
England, is of a
new species. The
delicate wing
veins can be
seen clearly.

Wing laced with veins

End of abdomen

Large eye

Wing veins

MODERN DRAGONFLY
One of the largest present-day
dragonflies is this species from
Borneo, with a wingspan of
6¼ in (16 cm). Although the
larvae of modern dragonflies
live in water, we cannot be
sure that this was true of
prehistoric dragonflies.

AGILE FLIERS
Modern dragonflies are fast, agile
fliers, and ancient dragonflies were
probably the same. A prehistoric
flying reptile would have had greater
trouble catching a dragonfly than
this fanciful engraving suggests.

TYPES OF INSECT

WE DO NOT KNOW exactly how many species, or type of insect there are, since scientists constantly discov new insects. There are about one million different named species. Each belongs to one of about 28 grou or orders, which are defined according to body structure and larval development.

Beetles, wasps, bees, and ants

About 350,000 species of beetles are described – they are the largest order of insects. Wasps, bees, and ants form the second largest order of insects, made up of about 125,000 species. The common feature in this order is a narrow "waist."

Jaws

STAC BEETL

Hard cases r midl

Fringed legs make swimming easier.

GREAT DIVING BEETLE

BEETLES

WINGS AND JAWS
The front pair of wings in beetles is hardened and forms a strong shield the folded hind wings. Some beetle such as stag beetles, have greatly enlarged jaws that look like horns.

DIFFERENT FOODS
Plants, fungi, insects, and dead animals are among the wide variety of beetle foods. Th great diving beetle lives in ponds. It is a fie predator which hunts tadpoles and small fi

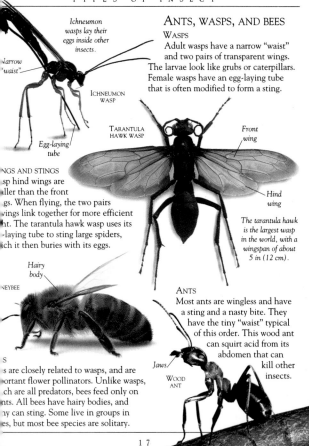

Ichneumon wasps lay their eggs inside other insects.

Narrow "waist"

ICHNEUMON WASP

Egg-laying tube

ANTS, WASPS, AND BEES

WASPS

Adult wasps have a narrow "waist" and two pairs of transparent wings. The larvae look like grubs or caterpillars. Female wasps have an egg-laying tube that is often modified to form a sting.

TARANTULA HAWK WASP

Front wing

Hind wing

The tarantula hawk is the largest wasp in the world, with a wingspan of about 5 in (12 cm).

NGS AND STINGS

sp hind wings are
ller than the front
gs. When flying, the two pairs
wings link together for more efficient
ht. The tarantula hawk wasp uses its
-laying tube to sting large spiders,
ich it then buries with its eggs.

Hairy body

NEYBEE

s are closely related to wasps, and are
ortant flower pollinators. Unlike wasps,
ch are all predators, bees feed only on
nts. All bees have hairy bodies, and
y can sting. Some live in groups in
es, but most bee species are solitary.

ANTS

Most ants are wingless and have a sting and a nasty bite. They have the tiny "waist" typical of this order. This wood ant can squirt acid from its abdomen that can kill other insects.

Jaws

WOOD ANT

Butterflies, moths, and flies

Two common insect orders are the two-winged flies and the butterflies and moths. Flies are distinctive because their second pair of wings is converted into balancing organs that look like drumsticks. Their young stages are maggots. Butterflies and moths have a coiled feeding tube, and their wings are covered in minute flattened scales. Butterfly and moth larvae are called caterpillars.

BUTTERFLIES AND MOTHS

CATERPILLARS

Although caterpillars' bodies are soft, they have an exoskeleton like other insects. Caterpillars grow at a very fast rate. They feed on leaves and have sharp jaws for slicing vegetation.

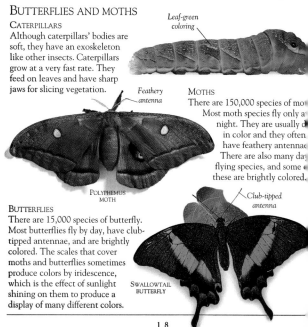

Leaf-green coloring

Feathery antenna

MOTHS

There are 150,000 species of moth. Most moth species fly only at night. They are usually dull in color and they often have feathery antennae. There are also many day-flying species, and some of these are brightly colored.

POLYPHEMUS MOTH

BUTTERFLIES

There are 15,000 species of butterfly. Most butterflies fly by day, have club-tipped antennae, and are brightly colored. The scales that cover moths and butterflies sometimes produce colors by iridescence, which is the effect of sunlight shining on them to produce a display of many different colors.

Club-tipped antenna

SWALLOWTAIL BUTTERFLY

FLIES

CRANE-FLY

Crane-flies live successfully all over the world. The larvae of some species of crane-fly are known as "leather-jackets," because their skin is so tough.

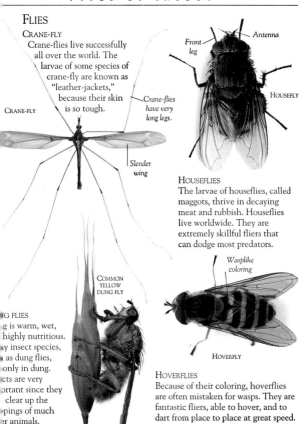

Front leg

Antenna

HOUSEFLY

CRANE-FLY

Crane-flies have very long legs.

Slender wing

HOUSEFLIES

The larvae of houseflies, called maggots, thrive in decaying meat and rubbish. Houseflies live worldwide. They are extremely skillful fliers that can dodge most predators.

COMMON YELLOW DUNG FLY

Wasplike coloring

HOVERFLY

...G FLIES

...g is warm, wet, ...highly nutritious. ...y insect species, ...as dung flies, ...only in dung. ...cts are very ...ortant since they ...clear up the ...pings of much ...er animals.

HOVERFLIES

Because of their coloring, hoverflies are often mistaken for wasps. They are fantastic fliers, able to hover, and to dart from place to place at great speed.

Bugs and other types

There are about 67,500 species of bug, the fifth-largest order of
insects. Bugs have a feeding tube folded back between the legs,
and most of them eat plant food. The other orders of insects
contain fewer species. Some of these orders are well known, suc
as fleas, cockroaches, dragonflies, and locusts.

BUGS

FEEDING TUBES

The mandibles (jaws) found in
most insects are modified into
needlelike tubes in bugs. The
bug pierces food with the
feeding tube and then
sucks up juices.

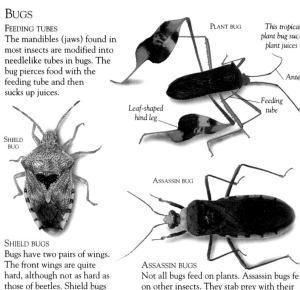

PLANT BUG

*This tropica
plant bug suc
plant juices*

Ant(

*Feeding
tube*

*Leaf-shaped
hind leg*

SHIELD
BUG

ASSASSIN BUG

SHIELD BUGS

Bugs have two pairs of wings.
The front wings are quite
hard, although not as hard as
those of beetles. Shield bugs
are so called because when
their wings are closed, they
look like colorful shields.

ASSASSIN BUGS

Not all bugs feed on plants. Assassin bugs fe
on other insects. They stab prey with their
feeding tube and then suck out the victim's
juices. Some South American assassin bugs
on the blood of humans and transmit diseas

Wing
buds

DESERT LOCUST
NYMPH

OTHER INSECT ORDERS

GRASSHOPPERS
The desert locust is a
member of the grasshopper
order. These insects eat
plants and have powerful
back legs for leaping.

MANTID

MANTIDS
Adults and mantid nymphs look
very similar. They both have very
large eyes and grasping front legs.
Mantids are colored like leaves
or flowers, so they can hide in them
as they wait for their prey to come near.

STICK
INSECT

COCKROACH

COCKROACHES
There are many fossils of cockroaches,
since they are one of the most ancient
orders of insects. Their front wings
overlap each other, instead
of meeting in the middle,
and the young stages
look like the adults.

DAMSELFLIES
The damselfly
and dragonfly order of
insects is millions of
years old, and fossils
show that some had a
wingspan of 2 ft (60 cm).
Nymphs are similar to
adults, but are adapted
for life underwater.

STICK INSECTS
This order is usually
found in the tropics. They look
like sticks with their long, slender
legs and bodies and feed only on
leaves. Their sticklike disguise
hides them from predators.

Wings
have many
veins.

METAMORPHOSIS

INSECTS GO THROUGH several stages of growth before
they become adults. This growing process is called
metamorphosis. There are two types of metamorphosi
complete and incomplete. Complete metamorphosis
has four growth stages – egg, larva, pupa, and adult.
Incomplete metamorphosis involves three stages – eg
nymph, and adult.

Incomplete metamorphosis

This growing process is a
gradual transformation. The
insects hatch from their
eggs looking like miniature
adults. These young insects
are called nymphs. As they
grow, they shed their skin
several times before they
reach the adult stage.

Clawed feet
hook onto
stem.

Wing
buds

Adult
head

Adu
head o
thora
emerg

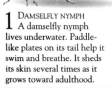

1 DAMSELFLY NYMPH
A damselfly nymph
lives underwater. Paddle-
like plates on its tail help it
swim and breathe. It sheds
its skin several times as it
grows toward adulthood.

2 HOLDING ON
When the nymph is
ready to change into an
adult it crawls out of the
water up a plant stem.

3 BREAKING OUT
The skin along th
back splits open and
the adult head and
thorax start to emerg

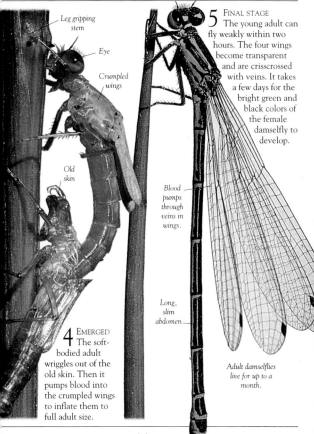

Leg gripping stem

Eye

Crumpled wings

Old skin

5 FINAL STAGE
The young adult can fly weakly within two hours. The four wings become transparent and are crisscrossed with veins. It takes a few days for the bright green and black colors of the female damselfly to develop.

Blood pumps through veins in wings.

Long, slim abdomen

4 EMERGED
The soft-bodied adult wriggles out of the old skin. Then it pumps blood into the crumpled wings to inflate them to full adult size.

Adult damselflies live for up to a month.

Complete metamorphosis

The four growth stages in a complete metamorphosis are egg, larva, pupa, and adult. The larva bears no resemblance to the adult it will become. During the pupa stage the larva makes the amazing transformation into an adult. Insects such as wasps, butterflies, beetles, and flies undergo complete metamorphosis.

1 LAYING EGGS
Butterflies lay eggs near leaves that caterpillars can eat when they hatch. Newly hatched caterpillars are too small to walk far to feed.

Eggshell

Egg

2 THE FIRST MEAL
When a caterpill emerges, the first meal it eats is usually its own eggshell. The eggshell provides the caterpillar wi valuable nutrients before i begins its diet of leaves.

Strong jaws slice food.

A caterpillar can increase its body weight by about 100 times in a few weeks.

3 GROWING
The caterpi chews up leaves and grows much bigger, shedd its skin several times. This gro prepares the caterpillar for the pup stage of its life.

A pupa is also known as a chrysalis.

Silk thread holds pupa in place.

A chrysalis often looks like a leaf for camouflage.

4 CHRYSALIS ACTIVITY

A pupa is like a busy factory. From the outside it looks still, but inside there is a great deal of activity. The caterpillar's organs turn into a milky liquid, and new butterfly organs grow rapidly in their place.

5 CHANGE COMPLETED

Once the metamorphosis is complete, the butterfly emerges from its pupa. It stretches its wet, crumpled wings. Before the butterfly is ready to fly, it must wait a couple of hours for its wings to expand and harden.

Empty pupa

Antenna

Wet, crumpled wings

Blood is pumped into the veins in the wings to expand them.

SWALLOWTAIL BUTTERFLY

Takes about eight weeks for this swallowtail butterfly to grow from egg to adult.

6 BUTTERFLY

The fully developed butterfly leads a totally different life from the caterpillar. While caterpillars eat leaves in order to grow, butterflies spend their time sipping nectar from flowers and seeking a mate.

HOW INSECTS MOVE

INSECTS MOVE using muscles which are attached to the inner surfaces of their hard outer skeleton. Many insects walk, but some larvae have no legs and have to crawl. Some insects swim, others jump, but most adult insects can fly and in this way they may travel long distances.

Legs

Insects use their legs for walking, running, jumping, and swimming. Many insects have legs modified for a number of other purposes. These include catching prey, holding a female when mating, producing songs, digging, fighting, and camouflage.

LEGS FOR SWIMMING
The water boatman has long, oar-shaped back legs, allowing the insect to "row" rapidly through water. The legs have flattened ends and a fringe of thick hairs. The front legs are short to grasp prey on the water surface.

LEGS FACTS
• Fairy flies, which live as parasites on the eggs of water insects, can "fly" underwater.
• Many butterflies walk on four legs; the front pair are used for tasting.
• The legless larvae of some parasitic wasps hitch a ride on a passing ant in order to enter an ant's nest.

1 PREPARING TO JUMP
The back legs of locusts are swollen and packed with strong muscles for jumping. Before leaping, a locust holds its back legs tightly under its body, near center of gravity. This is the best position for the legs to propel the insect high into the air.

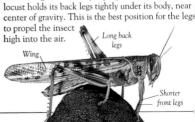

Long back legs

Wing

Shorter front legs

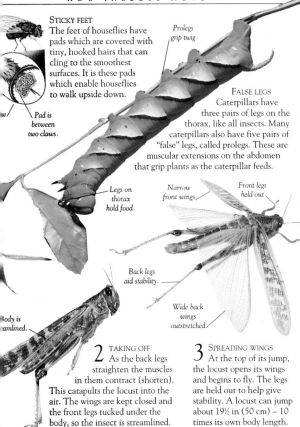

STICKY FEET

The feet of houseflies have pads which are covered with tiny, hooked hairs that can cling to the smoothest surfaces. It is these pads which enable houseflies to walk upside down.

Pad is between two claws.

Prolegs grip twig

Legs on thorax hold food.

FALSE LEGS

Caterpillars have three pairs of legs on the thorax, like all insects. Many caterpillars also have five pairs of "false" legs, called prolegs. These are muscular extensions on the abdomen that grip plants as the caterpillar feeds.

Narrow front wings

Front legs held out

Back legs aid stability.

Wide back wings outstretched

Body is streamlined.

2 TAKING OFF

As the back legs straighten the muscles in them contract (shorten). This catapults the locust into the air. The wings are kept closed and the front legs tucked under the body, so the insect is streamlined.

3 SPREADING WINGS

At the top of its jump, the locust opens its wings and begins to fly. The legs are held out to help give stability. A locust can jump about 19½ in (50 cm) – 10 times its own body length.

Wings and scales

Insect wings are a wide variety of shap
and sizes. They are used not just for fly
but also for attracting a mate or hiding
from predators. Most insects have t
pairs of wings, each with a netw
of veins to give strength. Flies
have only one pair of wings –
second pair is modified into s
balancing organs called halter
Small insects have few wing v
since their wings are so tiny.

EXPERT FLIERS
Dragonflies are among the
most accomplished fliers in
the insect world. They can
hover, fly fast or slow, change
direction rapidly, and even
fly backward. As they
maneuver, their two pairs
of wings beat independently
of each other.

WING FACTS

• The scales of
butterflies and moths
contain waste products
from the pupal stage.

• There is a hearing
organ in one of the
wing veins of green
lacewings for hearing
the shrieks of bats.

• Many species of
island insects are
wingless because of the
risk of being blown
out to sea.

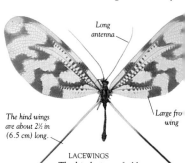

Long
antenna

Large fro
wing

The hind wings
are about 2½ in
(6.5 cm) long.

LACEWINGS
The hind wings of ribbon-
tail lacewings are modified into
long graceful streamers. Scientists are
not sure what these are for, but they may
act as stabilizers in flight, or even divert
predators from attacking the lacewing's body.
The lacewing's mottled patterns probably hel
conceal it in the dry, sandy places where it liv

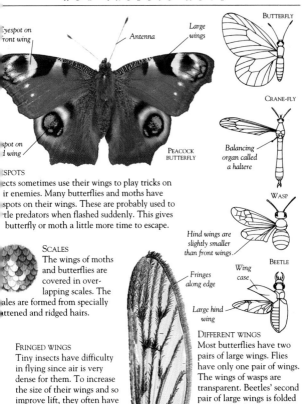

Eyespot on front wing

Antenna

Large wings

BUTTERFLY

spot on d wing

PEACOCK BUTTERFLY

CRANE-FLY

Balancing organ called a haltere

WASP

Hind wings are slightly smaller than front wings

BEETLE

Wing case

Fringes along edge

Large hind wing

SPOTS
ects sometimes use their wings to play tricks on ir enemies. Many butterflies and moths have spots on their wings. These are probably used to tle predators when flashed suddenly. This gives butterfly or moth a little more time to escape.

SCALES
The wings of moths and butterflies are covered in over-lapping scales. The ales are formed from specially ttened and ridged hairs.

FRINGED WINGS
Tiny insects have difficulty in flying since air is very dense for them. To increase the size of their wings and so improve lift, they often have fringes of hairs around the edges of the wings.

DIFFERENT WINGS
Most butterflies have two pairs of large wings. Flies have only one pair of wings. The wings of wasps are transparent. Beetles' second pair of large wings is folded away under the hardened first pair, or wing cases.

Flight

The ability to fly is one of the main reasons insects have survived for millions of years, and continue to flourish. Flight helps insects escape from danger. It also makes it easier to find food and new places to live. Sometimes insects fly thousands of miles to reach fresh food or warmer weather.

FLYING GROUPS
This African grasshopper has broad hind wings wh allow it to glide for long distances. Locusts are a ty of grasshopper that fly in huge groups when they need new food. Sometim as many as 100 million locusts fly together for hundreds of miles.

WARMING UP
An insect's flight muscles must be warm before the wings can be moved fast enough for flight. On cool mornings, insects like this shield bug shiver, vibrating their wings to warm themselves up.

Vibrating wings

1 PREPARING TO FLY
This cockchafer beetle prepares for flight by climbing to the top of a plant and facing into the wind. It may open and shut its elytra (wing cases) several times while warming up.

Elytra protect body.

2 OPENING THE WINC
The hardene elytra, which protect the fragile hin wings, beg to open. T antennae spread so t beetle can monitor the wind directio

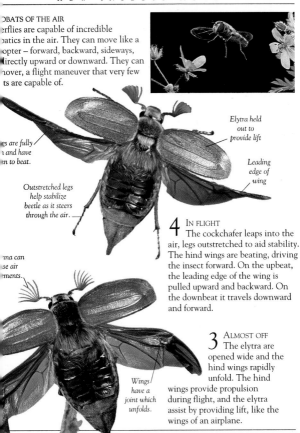

OBATS OF THE AIR
erflies are capable of incredible
atics in the air. They can move like a
opter – forward, backward, sideways,
irectly upward or downward. They can
over, a flight maneuver that very few
ts are capable of.

*Elytra held
out to
provide lift*

*gs are fully
n and have
n to beat.*

*Leading
edge of
wing*

*Outstretched legs
help stabilize
beetle as it steers
through the air.*

4 IN FLIGHT
The cockchafer leaps into the
air, legs outstretched to aid stability.
The hind wings are beating, driving
the insect forward. On the upbeat,
the leading edge of the wing is
pulled upward and backward. On
the downbeat it travels downward
and forward.

*nna can
se air
ements.*

3 ALMOST OFF
The elytra are
opened wide and the
hind wings rapidly
unfold. The hind
wings provide propulsion
during flight, and the elytra
assist by providing lift, like the
wings of an airplane.

*Wings
have a
joint which
unfolds.*

3 1

INSECT SENSES

INSECTS NEED to be fully aware of the world around them in order to survive. Although insects are tiny, some have keener senses than many larger animals. They can see colors and hear sounds that are undetectable to humans, as well as being able to detect smells from many miles away.

Sight

HEAD OF COMMON DARTER DRAGONFLY

There are two types of insect eyes – simple and compound. Simple eyes can probably detect only light and shade. Compound eyes have hundreds of lenses, giving their owner excellent vision.

SIMPLE EYES
Caterpillars never need to look far for their plant food – they are constantly surrounded by it. Because of this, they do not need sharp eyesight. They can manage perfectly well with a group of simple eyes.

GOOD VISION
The eyes of dragonflies take up m of their head. This allows them t see what's in front, above, below, and behind them all at the same time. Dragonflies use their excellent sight and agile flight to catch prey.

Simple eyes

COMMON DARTER DRAGONFLY

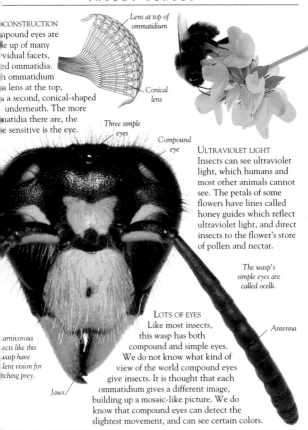

CONSTRUCTION
Compound eyes are made up of many individual facets, called ommatidia. Each ommatidium has a lens at the top, and a second, conical-shaped lens underneath. The more ommatidia there are, the more sensitive is the eye.

Lens at top of ommatidium

Conical lens

Three simple eyes

Compound eye

ULTRAVIOLET LIGHT
Insects can see ultraviolet light, which humans and most other animals cannot see. The petals of some flowers have lines called honey guides which reflect ultraviolet light, and direct insects to the flower's store of pollen and nectar.

The wasp's simple eyes are called ocelli.

Antenna

Carnivorous insects like this wasp have excellent vision for catching prey.

Jaws

LOTS OF EYES
Like most insects, this wasp has both compound and simple eyes. We do not know what kind of view of the world compound eyes give insects. It is thought that each ommatidium gives a different image, building up a mosaic-like picture. We do know that compound eyes can detect the slightest movement, and can see certain colors.

33

Smelling, hearing, and touching

The bodies of insects are covered in short hairs which are connected to the nervous system. These hairs can feel, or "hear," vibrations in the air due to either sound or movement. Some ha are modified to detect smells and flavors. Sensory hairs are often found on the antennae, but also occur on the feet and mouthpa

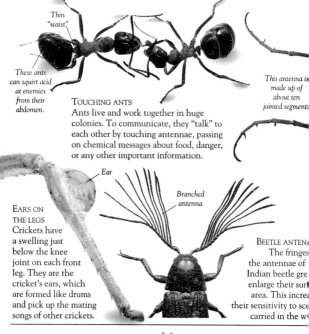

Thin "waist"

These ants can squirt acid at enemies from their abdomen.

This antenna is made up of about ten jointed segments

TOUCHING ANTS
Ants live and work together in huge colonies. To communicate, they "talk" to each other by touching antennae, passing on chemical messages about food, danger, or any other important information.

Ear

Branched antenna

EARS ON
THE LEGS
Crickets have a swelling just below the knee joint on each front leg. They are the cricket's ears, which are formed like drums and pick up the mating songs of other crickets.

BEETLE ANTEN
The fringes
the antennae of
Indian beetle gre
enlarge their sur
area. This incre
their sensitivity to sc
carried in the w

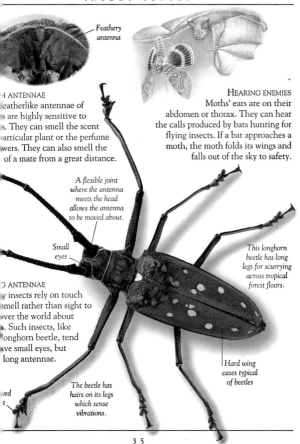

Feathery
antenna

H ANTENNAE
eatherlike antennae of
s are highly sensitive to
s. They can smell the scent
articular plant or the perfume
wers. They can also smell the
of a mate from a great distance.

HEARING ENEMIES
Moths' ears are on their
abdomen or thorax. They can hear
the calls produced by bats hunting for
flying insects. If a bat approaches a
moth, the moth folds its wings and
falls out of the sky to safety.

A flexible joint
where the antenna
meets the head
allows the antenna
to be moved about.

Small
eyes

This longhorn
beetle has long
legs for scurrying
across tropical
forest floors.

G ANTENNAE
y insects rely on touch
smell rather than sight to
ver the world about
. Such insects, like
onghorn beetle, tend
ve small eyes, but
long antennae.

Hard wing
cases typical
of beetles

ed
t

The beetle has
hairs on its legs
which sense
vibrations.

Jaws chew leaf.

Caterpillar holds leaf with its legs.

HOW INSECTS FEED

INSECTS HAVE complex mouthpar. The insects that chew their foo have a pair of strong jaws for chopping, a smaller pair of jaws for holding food, and two pairs of sensory organs, called palps, for tasting. Some insects drink only liquid food and have specia tubular mouthparts like a straw.

Chewing

Predatory, chewing insects need sharp, pointed jaws for stabbing, holding, and chopping up their struggling prey. Inse that chew plants have blunter jaws for grinding their food.

PLANT CHEWER
A caterpillar needs powerful jaws to bite into plant material. Their jaws are armed with teeth that overlap when they close. Some caterpillars' jaws are modified into grinding plates for mashing up the toughest leaves.

THRUSTING JAWS
Dragonfly larvae have pincer the end of a hinged plate folc under the head. When catch prey, the plate unfolds, shoot forward, and the pincers grab prey. Toothed jaws in the he reduce the victim to mincem

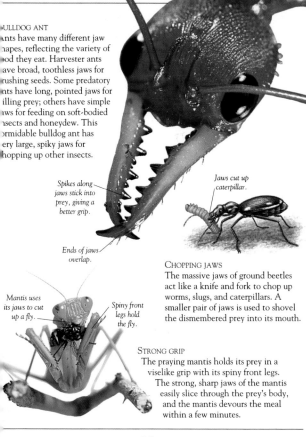

BULLDOG ANT

Ants have many different jaw
shapes, reflecting the variety of
food they eat. Harvester ants
have broad, toothless jaws for
crushing seeds. Some predatory
ants have long, pointed jaws for
killing prey; others have simple
jaws for feeding on soft-bodied
insects and honeydew. This
formidable bulldog ant has
very large, spiky jaws for
chopping up other insects.

*Spikes along
jaws stick into
prey, giving a
better grip.*

*Ends of jaws
overlap.*

*Jaws cut up
caterpillar.*

CHOPPING JAWS
The massive jaws of ground beetles
act like a knife and fork to chop up
worms, slugs, and caterpillars. A
smaller pair of jaws is used to shovel
the dismembered prey into its mouth.

*Mantis uses
its jaws to cut
up a fly.*

*Spiny front
legs hold
the fly.*

STRONG GRIP
The praying mantis holds its prey in a
viselike grip with its spiny front legs.
The strong, sharp jaws of the mantis
easily slice through the prey's body,
and the mantis devours the meal
within a few minutes.

Drinking

For many insects, the main way of feeding is by drinking. The
most nutritious foods to drink are nectar and blood. Nectar is
rich in sugar, and blood is packed with proteins. Some insects
drink by sucking through strawlike mouthparts. Others have
spongelike mouthparts with which they mop up liquids.

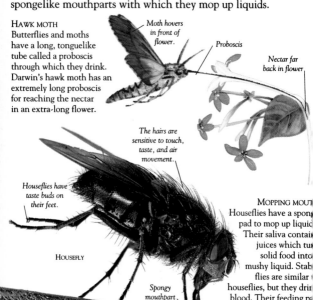

HAWK MOTH
Butterflies and moths
have a long, tonguelike
tube called a proboscis
through which they drink.
Darwin's hawk moth has an
extremely long proboscis
for reaching the nectar
in an extra-long flower.

Moth hovers in front of flower.

Proboscis

Nectar far back in flower

The hairs are sensitive to touch, taste, and air movement.

Houseflies have taste buds on their feet.

HOUSEFLY

Spongy mouthpart

MOPPING MOUT
Houseflies have a spong
pad to mop up liquid
Their saliva contain
juices which tu
solid food into
mushy liquid. Stab
flies are similar
houseflies, but they drin
blood. Their feeding pa
has teeth which cut a
animal's skin
make it blee

Rostrum

The saliva kills the prey and dissolves its insides, which the bug drinks.

Assassin bug

Antenna

ROSTRUM

Assassin bugs pierce prey with needlelike stylets enclosed in a sheath called a rostrum. The stylets form a double tube so that saliva goes down one side while food comes up the other.

...ILED PROBOSCIS
...en the proboscis of
...terflies and moths is not
...use it is coiled beneath
... head. Different
...cies have different
...gths of proboscis.
... longest known
...boscis belongs to a
...dagascan moth, and is
...ut 13 in (33 cm) long.

Long proboscis

Coiled proboscis

...RSEFLIES
...t horseflies have
...felike jaws to make
...mals bleed. But this
...ous oriental horsefly
...short, stout mouthparts
...ed on blood, and a
...slender proboscis to
...ect nectar from flowers.

COURTSHIP, BIRTH, AND GROWTH

REPRODUCTION is hazardous for insects. A female must first mate with a male of her own species and lay eggs where the newly hatched young can feed. The larvae must shed their skin several times as they grow. All this time the insects must avoid being eaten.

The light is produced by a chemical reaction.

GUIDING LIGHT
Glowworms are the wing[...] females of certain beetle[...] species. They attract ma[...] by producing a light nea[...] the tip of their abdomen[...] Some species flash a distinctive code to attra[...] the correct males.

Courtship and mating

Males and females use special signals to ensure that their chosen mate is the right species. Courtship usually involves using scents, but may include color displays, dancing, caressing, and even gifts.

Butterflies find the scented chemicals, called pheromones, very attractive.

COURTSHIP FLIGHTS
Butterflies may recognize their own species by sight, but scent is more reliable. Butterfly courtship involves dancing flights with an exchange of scented chemical signals specific to each species.

MATING DANGER
Mating between some insect species may last for several hours, with the male gripping the female's abdomen with claspers. This keeps other males away, but the pair are vulnerable to predators at this time.

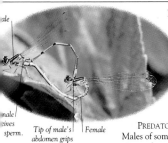

DAMSELFLIES

When mating, a male damselfly grips a female's neck with the tip of his abdomen. She receives a packet of sperm from a pouch near his legs; he continues to hold her neck while she lays eggs. This prevents other males from mating with her.

male receives sperm.

Tip of male's abdomen grips female.

Female

PREDATORS MATING

Males of some predatory species, such as empid flies, give the female a meal of a dead insect when mating so they are not eaten themselves. Some males trick the female. They give an empty parcel, and mate while the female opens it.

Female

MATING ASIAN SWALLOWTAIL BUTTERFLIES

UNNATURAL BEHAVIOR

It is often said that a female mantis eats the male while he is mating with her. But this probably happens only when the mantises are in captivity and their behavior is not natural.

Male

Eggs and egg-laying

Insects use up a lot of energy producing eggs. To make sure this energy is not wasted, insects have many ways of protecting their eggs from predators. A few species of insect stay with their eggs to protect them until the larvae hatch. Some insects lay their eggs underground with a supply of food waiting for the newly hatched larvae. Most insects lay their eggs either in or near food, so the young larvae do not have to travel far to eat.

The egg-laying tube, also known as an ovipositor, drills into the wood.

The ovipositor is longer than the ichneumon's body.

ICHNEUMON W.
The larvae of ichneun
wasps are parasites, wh
means they feed on ot
living creatures. Wh
finding a host for its egg,
adult ichneumon detects
vibrations of a beetle g
gnawing inside a tree tru
The wasp drives its e
laying tube into the tru
until it finds the grub.
egg is laid on the grub, wh
then provides food for
wasp larva when it hatcl

SUITABLE FOOD

Butterflies desert their eggs once they are laid. Different butterflies lay their eggs on different plants, depending on what the larvae eat. The Malay lacewing butterfly lays its eggs on vine tendrils.

Wasp carrying beetle to nest

CARING EARWIGS
~ale earwig looks
~er eggs, licking
~ regularly to
~ them clean.
~ the nymphs
~h, she feeds
~ until they
~g enough to
~ve the nest.

Beetles are stored in underground nest.

Earwig eggs

HUNTING WASPS

Most species of hunting wasp collect soft-bodied prey, such as caterpillars or spiders, for their grubs. But the weevil-hunting wasp collects adult beetles, which it stings and then stores in a tunnel as food for its larvae.

~al ~
~l ~

Beetles mold dung into balls.

Beetle fills tunnel with dung as food for newly hatched grubs.

~ BEETLES
~nales and females of some dung
~ species work together to dig an underground
~l with smaller tunnels branching off it. A female
~n egg in each of the smaller tunnels and fills them
~nimal dung, which the beetle grubs will feed on.

INSECT EGG FACTS

• Whitefly eggs have stalks that extract water from leaves.

• Tsetse flies develop their eggs internally and lay mature larvae.

• Green lacewing eggs have long stalks, making them difficult for predators to eat.

Birth and growth

Newborn aphid

As an insect grows from egg to adult it sheds its
skin several times to produce a larger exoskeleton.
While this new skin hardens the insect is soft
and vulnerable. Insects have many life-cycle
adaptations to protect their soft young stages.

EGGS LARVA PUPA ADULT LADYBUG

LADYBUG GROWTH
Ladybugs and all other beetles go through a complete
metamorphosis. An adult ladybug lays its eggs on a
plant where small insects called aphids feed. Ladybug
larvae eat aphids and shed their skin three times as
they grow. The colorful adult emerges from the dull
resting stage, or pupa.

APHIDS
Female aphids can
reproduce without m
They give birth to liv
young rather than la
and each female may
about 100 offspring. '
newborn aphids can
birth after only a few

FROTHY PROTEC
Spittlebugs are soft-bodied bug
aphids. A spittlebug nymph pro
a frothy liquid from its anus
froth protects the nymph
drying out, and also h
from pred

Frothy hideaway

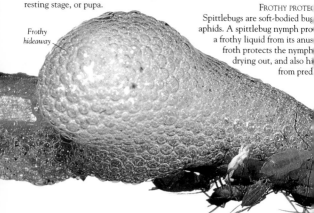

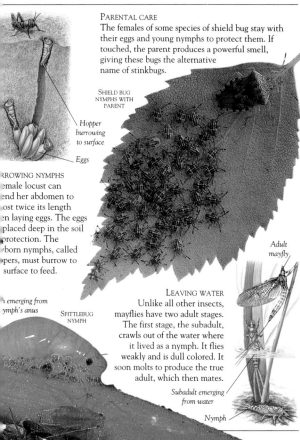

PARENTAL CARE

The females of some species of shield bug stay with their eggs and young nymphs to protect them. If touched, the parent produces a powerful smell, giving these bugs the alternative name of stinkbugs.

SHIELD BUG NYMPHS WITH PARENT

Hopper burrowing to surface

Eggs

BURROWING NYMPHS

The female locust can extend her abdomen to almost twice its length when laying eggs. The eggs are placed deep in the soil for protection. The newborn nymphs, called hoppers, must burrow to the surface to feed.

...h emerging from ...nymph's anus

SPITTLEBUG NYMPH

LEAVING WATER

Unlike all other insects, mayflies have two adult stages. The first stage, the subadult, crawls out of the water where it lived as a nymph. It flies weakly and is dull colored. It soon molts to produce the true adult, which mates.

Adult mayfly

Subadult emerging from water

Nymph

Survival of the young

Predators eagerly hunt insect larvae since many are slow-moving, soft, and nutritious. To ensure survival, most insect species produce large numbers of young which grow rapidly. Most insect larvae are defenseless and have developed special ways of hiding from predators. But many insect larvae are fierce predators themselves, consuming other creatures for nourishment as they grow.

Grub in pupal cell

Caterpillar rears up when threatened

WELL HIDDEN
The larvae of chafer beetles live underground, safely hidden from most predators. The larvae, or grubs, may take many weeks to develop. They then produce a cell of hardened soil in which they will change into an adult.

Fearsome "face"

True legs

Sharp spines

Proleg

SPINY LARVA
Mexican bean beetle larvae eat leaves and develop rapidly. They are covered with long, branched spines which may deter birds and other predators from attacking them.

SCARY DISPLAY
Caterpillars are a favorite food of birds. Some caterpillars try to hide to stay safe. But if the puss moth caterpillar is threatened, it puts on a startling display which can frighten off birds

WATER LARVA

Stone-fly larvae live in cold water and grow slowly, spending about three years as a larva. They are slow-moving and hide from predators under rocks and among plants.

...HT FEEDER

...mormon butterfly ...rpillar feeds in the ... of night to avoid being ... by predators. In less than eight ...rs it will chew away a leaf which ...ore than twice its own length. ...ng the day it rests as ...nspicuously as possible.

...a more frightening ...y, the caterpillar ...s these "tails" as if ...ey were stings.

SOFT BODIES

Young mantids are fierce predators. The body of some species resembles a flower. This disguise helps them to go unnoticed by prey, and also by predators such as birds.

Eye

Leg

Pink, flowerlike body

Legs are striped pink and green.

NESTS AND SOCIETIES

MOST INSECTS lead solitary lives, but some, particularly wasps, ants, bees, and termites, live in societies which are sometimes very ordered. There are queens, kings, workers, and soldiers. Each of these has particular jobs to do. Social insects live in nests which are often elaborate, where they protect each other and rear their young.

TROPICAL WASP NEST MADE OF CHEWED-UP PLANT FIBERS

Wasps, ants, and bees

The nest is cemented together with wasp saliva.

These insects produce a wide range of nests. So are small with only a few dozen members, while larger nests may contain thousand insects. Most have a single queen, and a the nest members are her offspring.

ANTS
A species of African tree ant builds its nest from fragments of plants and soil to produce a substance like dark cement. The ants live on a diet of honeydew that they get from aphids. The aphids feed on the sap of leaves in the tree tops and discharge the honeydew from their rear ends.

BEES
A bumblebee queen sta her nest alone in spring a hole in the ground. S makes cells for her eggs of wax. She also makes wax pot which she fills with honey for food.

The queen uses her antennae to measure the cells as she builds them.

A NEW START
European wasp colonies die out each [win]ter. In spring a queen begins a new nest of [pa]per" made with chewed-up wood. She makes [ne]w cells for her eggs, building walls around [the] cells to shield them.

[Un]finished nest

2 PROTECTIVE LAYERS
The queen builds more and more paper layers around the cells. The layers will protect the larvae from cold winds as well as from predators. The queen leaves an entrance hole at the bottom.

Entrance hole

3 HARD-WORKING FAMILY
The first brood the queen rears become workers, [g]athering food for more larvae and expanding the [n]est. By summer, a nest may have 500 wasps, all [c]ollecting caterpillars for the larvae. A large nest [m]ay be as much as 18 in (45 cm) in diameter.

INSIDE THE NEST
The queen lays a single egg in each cell. When the larvae hatch they stay in their cell and the queen feeds them with pieces of caterpillar.

Termite nests

Termites have the most complex insect societies. Their elaborate nests, which may be in wood or underground, last for several years. Each nest has a single large queen and king, which are served by specialized small workers and large soldiers. Termites feed and protect each other, and one generation will help raise the next generation of offspring.

QUEEN TERMITE
In a termite society, the que lays all the eggs. She is too f move, so the workers bring f to her. The queen lays 30,00 eggs each day and, as she lay them, the workers carry ther to special chambers for reari

Layers of "umbrellas"

NEST DEFENDERS
Termite soldiers fight enemies th attack the nest. Most termite spe have soldiers with enlarged head and powerful jaws. In some speci each soldier's head has a snout th squirts poison at invaders.

STRANGE NEST
The function of the "umbrellas" on this Africa nest is a mystery to scientists. The termite spe that build this type of nest live underground. I "umbrella" is damaged, it does not get repaire but a new one may be built.

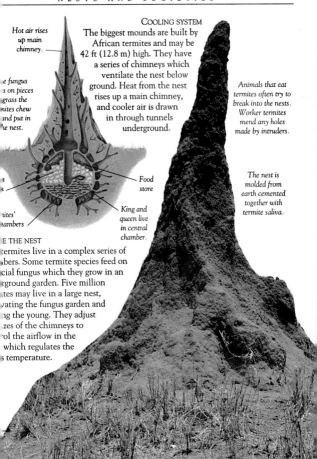

Hot air rises up main chimney.

e fungus s on pieces grass the mites chew nd put in he nest.

COOLING SYSTEM

The biggest mounds are built by African termites and may be 42 ft (12.8 m) high. They have a series of chimneys which ventilate the nest below ground. Heat from the nest rises up a main chimney, and cooler air is drawn in through tunnels underground.

Animals that eat termites often try to break into the nests. Worker termites mend any holes made by intruders.

Food store

King and queen live in central chamber.

The nest is molded from earth cemented together with termite saliva.

ites' ambers

E THE NEST

termites live in a complex series of bers. Some termite species feed on cial fungus which they grow in an rground garden. Five million tes may live in a large nest, vating the fungus garden and g the young. They adjust zes of the chimneys to rol the airflow in the which regulates the s temperature.

HUNTING AND HIDING

SOME INSECT SPECIES are deadly hunters, killing prey with poisonous stings and sharp jaws. Insects are also hunted by a huge number of animals. To hide from predators, many insects have developed special disguises and patterns of behavior.

Hunting insects

About one-third of insect species are carnivorous (they eat meat). Some species eat decaying meat and dung, but most carnivorous insects hunt for their food.

KILLER BEETLE
Some insects are easily recognized as predators. The large jaws of this African ground beetle indicate that it is a hunter and its long legs show that it can run fast after its insect prey.

KILLER WASPS
There are many types of hunting wasp. Most adult hunting wasps vegetarians – they hunt prey only as food for their larvae. Each hunting wasp species a particular type of prey. The weevil-hunting wasp hunts only a type of beetle called a weevil.

ESSENTIAL INSECTS

Ants are the most important carnivores on Earth. They eat huge numbers of other insects, which helps keep the insect population from becoming too plentiful. Ants in turn are eaten by other animals, such as birds and lizards.

Wasp cocoons

PARASITES

The larvae of many species of wasp are parasites, which means they feed and grow inside another insect's body. This caterpillar has had about 50 wasp larvae feeding inside it. The larvae are pupating on the caterpillar's back. Soon they will hatch as adult wasps.

Wasp uses its antennae and sight to find cockroaches.

SPECIALIST HUNTER

Many predatory insects specialize on one particular type of prey. This jewel wasp hunts only cockroaches, which it uses as food for its larvae. The adult wasp is not carnivorous – it feeds on the nectar in flowers.

ROVE BEETLE

Some rove beetles specialize in feeding on springtails. To catch such elusive prey the beetle can flick out a long, sticky "tongue" to pull an unwary springtail into its mouth.

Beetle raises tail before attacking prey.

Camouflage

Insects whose body coloring matches their background are almo
impossible to see. This method of hiding is known as camouflag
One of the first rules of successful camouflage is to keep still, sin
movement can betray an insect to a sharp-eyed predator. Some
insects use another type of camouflage called
disruptive coloration. They disguise
their body by breaking up its
shape with stripes and
blocks of color.

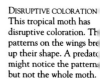

GRASSY DISGUISE
The stripe-winged
grasshopper can be
heard singing in
meadow grasses, but
its camouflaged body
is very hard to spot.

*Grasshopper kicks
any attackers with
its back legs.*

DISRUPTIVE COLORATION
This tropical moth has
disruptive coloration. Th
patterns on the wings bre
up their shape. A predato
might notice the pattern
but not the whole moth.

LOOKING DISTASTEFUL
This treehopper has
twiglike extensions on
its thorax and abdomen.
It looks like an inedible
piece of wood, so
hunters are likely to
overlook it.

*Extensi
on thor*

Wing

STILL HUNTER
Insect predators use camouflage so
their prey cannot see them. The
brown coloring of this mantid
perfectly matches the brown leaf
on which it sits. It completely
surprises any prey which
comes within
striking distance.

*Because of its brown
coloring, the Indian
leaf butterfly can rest
only beside decaying,
dried-out leaves.*

Midvein on
real leaf

...ntis is
...d to
...ot.

Butterfly's
head

Wing of
butterfly

LEAF MIMIC
It is almost impossible
to distinguish the Indian
leaf butterfly from the other
leaves where it rests. It looks
just like a decaying leaf,
complete with leaflike veins
and mock fungus spots.

Bottom of wings
are narrow to
look like stalk of
real leaf.

Marking like
midvein of real
leaf

Warning coloration

Birds, mammals, and other intelligent
predators learn through experience that
some insects are poisonous or harmful.
Such insects do not camouflage themselves.
Instead they have brightly colored bodies
which warn predators that they have an
unpleasant taste or a nasty sting. The
most common warning colors are red,
yellow, and black. Any insect with those
colors is probably poisonous.

BASKER MOTH
Moths that fly by day
often brightly colore
particularly when the
taste unpleasant. The
red, yellow, and blac
coloring of this baske
moth tells birds that
not a tasty meal.

PAINFUL REMINDER
The saddle-back caterpillar is
eye-catching with its vivid
coloring and grotesque
appearance. No young bird
would ever forget the
caterpillar if it tried a
mouthful of the poisonous,
stinging spines.

*Poisonous
spines*

*Vivid green
coloring
across back*

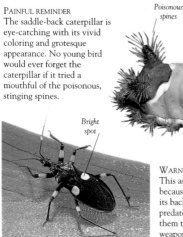

*Bright
spot*

WARNING SPOTS
This assassin bug is easily seen
because of the two bright spots on
its back. These bold markings warn
predators that there is a reason for
them to stay away. The bug's
weapon is a needle-sharp beak
which can give a very painful bite.

EYESPOTS
This silkmoth is camouflaged when its wings are closed. But when attacked by a predator, the moth flashes the eyespots on its hind wings. This startles the attacker briefly, and may give the moth time to escape.

Camouflaged front wings

Eyespot

POISONOUS BODY
This grasshopper tastes horrible. It gets its terrible flavor from eating poisonous plants and storing the poisons in its body. The yellow and black stripes advertise its unpleasantness to birds and other predators.

Grasshopper uses the spines on its legs to grip plants.

...es are black to ...end with rest of coloring.

Mimicry

Predators usually avoid preying on dangerous animals. Many harmless insects take advantage of this by mimicking harmful creatures. Mimicking insects copy a dangerous animal's body shape and coloring. They also behave like the animal they're copying to make the disguise more convincing. Inedible objects, such as twigs and thorns, are also mimicked by insects.

The treehoppers move only when they need a fresh source of food.

Markings make head resemble alligator's head.

Real eye of bug

ALLIGATOR MIMIC
Scientists can often only guess at the reasons for the strange look and behavior of some animals. It is not known why this tree-living bug looks like a tiny alligator. Perhaps its appearance briefly startles monkey predators, giving the bug time to fly off to safety.

HORNET MIMIC
The hornet moth looks very like the large wasp called a hornet. When flying, it even behaves like a hornet. Many insects get protection by mimicking wasps – birds avoid them because they might sting.

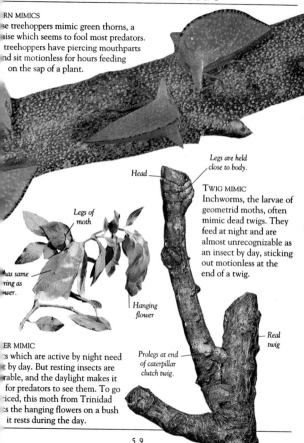

RN MIMICS
se treehoppers mimic green thorns, a
uise which seems to fool most predators.
treehoppers have piercing mouthparts
nd sit motionless for hours feeding
on the sap of a plant.

Legs are held
close to body.

Head

TWIG MIMIC
Inchworms, the larvae of
geometrid moths, often
mimic dead twigs. They
feed at night and are
almost unrecognizable as
an insect by day, sticking
out motionless at the
end of a twig.

Legs of
moth

has same
ring as
wer.

Hanging
flower

Real
twig

Prolegs at end
of caterpillar
clutch twig.

ER MIMIC
s which are active by night need
t by day. But resting insects are
rable, and the daylight makes it
for predators to see them. To go
iced, this moth from Trinidad
s the hanging flowers on a bush
it rests during the day.

WHERE INSECTS LIVE

INSECTS LIVE everywhere there is warmth and moisture. Many of the one million or more species have specialized habitat requirements. They can live only in particular places, and easily become extinct when humans change or destroy their surroundings. Other species are able to adapt to changing conditions; these adaptable insects often become pests.

TEMPERATE WOODLAND
The varied plant life and complex structure of temperate woodland provides insects with many different habitats. Trees, shrubs, and herbs all have flowers, fruits, and buds for insects to feed on, as well as stems and roots for insects to bore into.

GRASSLANDS AND HEATHLANDS
These habitats offer little shelter from bad weather. But they warm up quickly in the sun, and have a rich variety of flowering plants.

TOWNS AND GARDENS
Hundreds of insect species take
advantage of human habitats.
Insects find food and shelter in our
roofs, cellars, food stores, kitchens,
garbage cans, farms, and in our
flower-filled gardens.

DESERTS, CAVES, AND SOIL
These are inhospitable habitats.
Food and water are scarce in
deserts. Caves are dark and cold.
It is hard for insects to move and
communicate in dense soil.

TROPICAL FORESTS
This is the richest habitat
for insect species. Thousands
of species of plants provide
countless niches for insects
to live in, from treetop fruits
to dead leaves and twigs on
the ground.

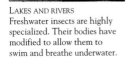

LAKES AND RIVERS
Freshwater insects are highly
specialized. Their bodies have
modified to allow them to
swim and breathe underwater.

TEMPERATE WOODLAND

ABOUT THE HABITAT 64
OAK TREE 66
TREE CANOPY 68
WOODLAND BUTTERFLIES 70
TREE TRUNKS AND BRANCHES 72
GROUND LEVEL 74

ABOUT THE HABITAT

FIELD SCA
FLOW

TEMPERATE WOODLANDS are often dominated by one tree species, such as oak, which is deciduous (the trees lose their leaves in winter). The types of insect found, and their numbers, will vary with the seasons, as well as with the types of tree species in the woodlands.

DRAINING
Forests in wetlands have many different plant species. But people often drain this habitat because it is good for farming. Draining kills plants such as milk-parsley, the only plant the English swallowtail butterfly will breed on. This beautiful insect is now rarely seen.

+1.4

Although the English swallowtail will lay eggs only on milk-parsley, adults eat a variety of flowers.

he woodland edge
ports the greatest
mber of insect species.

ach pair of blue
needs about 5,000
erpillars to feed to
eir chicks.

n Britain, over 280
cies of insect live on
tive oak trees.

emperate rainforests
the northwestern
ited States are
appearing faster than
pical rainforests.

*Bumblebees are
very common in
woodlands.*

+2

FLOWERS
Woodlands contain
many types of flower.
These attract various species
of insect, such as bumblebees,
which nest in the ground in
animal burrows and pollinate
many woodland flowers.

*Vaporer moth
caterpillar is covered
with tufts of hair.*

VAPORER MOTH CATERPILLAR
This attractive caterpillar eats the
leaves of many different trees in
Europe and North America.
It will also attack
rosebushes and
heather plants.

*Processionary
caterpillars are
covered in
poisonous hairs.*

PROCESSIONS
Conifer forests have
fewer types of plant and
animal than deciduous
forests, although some, such as
processionary moth caterpillars, can be
common. These are named for their habit
of following each other head to tail.

OAK TREE

IN NORTH AMERICA and Europe, oak
trees support a rich variety of insects.
There are insects living on every part
of the oak tree – the leaves,
buds, flowers, fruits, wood,
bark, and on decaying
leaves and branches. All
these insects provide food
for the many birds and other
animals found in oak woodland.

OAK TREE

GREEN OAK
TORTRIX MOTH

CATERPILLAR

GREEN OAK TORTRIX

The green wings of the green
oak tortrix moth camouflage
the moth when it rests on a
leaf. Green oak tortrix
caterpillars are extremely
common on oak trees.
The caterpillars hide from
hungry predators by rolling
themselves up in a leaf.

+2

+1.25

Leaf ro
around g
oak torti
caterpi

Mine

MAKING A TUNNEL

The caterpillars of some sm
moths tunnel between the
upper and lower surfaces of
leaf. They eat the green tiss
between these surfaces as t
tunnel, and leave a see-
through trail called a mine

*Chalcid wasp
larvae have eaten
the gall wasp larvae*

GALLS

Oak trees have many tiny
growths called galls. Galls are
grown by the tree around eggs
laid by gall wasps. When the eggs
hatch, the gall provides food and shelter
~~f~~or up to 30 wasp larvae. Parasitic wasps called
~~chal~~cid wasps sometimes burrow inside galls and lay
~~their~~ eggs beside the gall wasp eggs. When the
~~chal~~cid larvae hatch they eat the gall wasp larvae.

CHALCID
WASP ON
GALL

WEEVILS
~~Aco~~rns are used as food by
~~nut~~ weevils. They drill a
~~hole~~ in an acorn with their
~~long~~, thin snout, and then
~~lay t~~heir eggs inside. The
~~larva~~e feed inside the
~~acorn~~, and this turns
~~the~~ acorn
~~blac~~k.

*Black
acorn*

ACORNS

Antenna

NUT WEEVIL

TREE CANOPY

THE UPPER BRANCHES and leaves
of a tree are like a living green
umbrella, forming a canopy over
the lower plants. Countless
insects find their food in the
canopy and they are food for
many different birds.

*Inchworm
on leaf*

*Silken thread
suspends
inchworm.*

INCHWORMS
Some young birds like
to feed on inchworms,
the caterpillars of
Geometrid moths.
When in danger, inchworm
can drop from a leaf and ha
below by a silken thread.

*Very long antennae help
the cricket find its way
in the dark. They also alert
the cricket to the approach
of an enemy.*

*Compound
eye*

OAK BUSH CRICKETS
At night, male oak bush crickets drum
on leaves with their feet so that a
female oak bush cricket, like this one,
knows where to find a mate. The
cricket's green body blends in well
with its leafy surroundings.

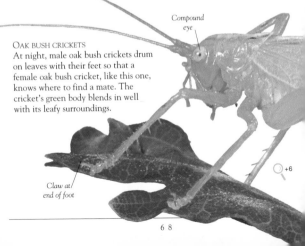

*Claw at
end of foot*

+6

Wasps kill insects that destroy plants and fruit.

...SPS
...ealthy
...odland has a
...ance of prey
... predators. Wasps grow up on a diet
...hewed caterpillars collected in the
... canopy. In summer a wasp nest
... contain several hundred wasps.

Claw on
end of foot
for gripping
surfaces

EUROPEAN
WASP

+2.7

...ong back
...s can be
...d to kick
...nemies.

MALE PURPLE
EMPEROR AT REST

Camouflaged
underside of
wings

–.5

PURPLE EMPEROR
The territory of a male
purple emperor is often at
the top of the tallest tree in
a wood. If a rival male enters
another male's territory, the
two fight in midair, batting
wings until one gives in.

MALE PURPLE
EMPEROR

Wings are
normally
dark brown.

It is only when wings
are at a certain angle
to the light that they
appear to be purple.

WOODLAND BUTTERFLIES

THE RICH VARIETY of habitats in woodland
supports many butterfly species.
Some live in the canopy; others
feed on low shrubs. But most
butterflies need sunshine and can be
found on flowers in sunny clearings

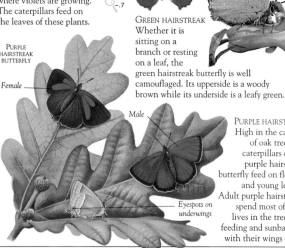

SILVER-WASHED FRITILLARY
This butterfly lays its eggs
in cracks in the bark of
mossy tree trunks, close to
where violets are growing.
The caterpillars feed on
the leaves of these plants.

Brown upperside

GREEN HAIRSTREAK
Whether it is
sitting on a
branch or resting
on a leaf, the
green hairstreak butterfly is well
camouflaged. Its upperside is a woody
brown while its underside is a leafy green.

Gree underside

PURPLE HAIRSTREAK BUTTERFLY

Female

Male

Eyespots on underwings

PURPLE HAIRSTREAK
High in the canopy
of oak trees the
caterpillars of the
purple hairstreak
butterfly feed on flowers
and young leaves.
Adult purple hairstreaks
spend most of their
lives in the treetops,
feeding and sunbathing
with their wings open

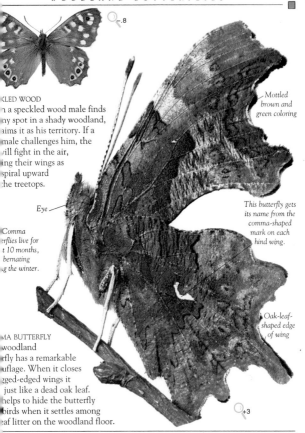

~.8

KLED WOOD
n a speckled wood male finds
ny spot in a shady woodland,
aims it as his territory. If a
male challenges him, the
ill fight in the air,
ing their wings as
spiral upward
he treetops.

*Mottled
brown and
green coloring*

Eye

*This butterfly gets
its name from the
comma-shaped
mark on each
hind wing.*

Comma
*rflies live for
t 10 months,
bernating
g the winter.*

*Oak-leaf-
shaped edge
of wing*

MA BUTTERFLY
woodland
rfly has a remarkable
uflage. When it closes
ged-edged wings it
just like a dead oak leaf.
helps to hide the butterfly
birds when it settles among
af litter on the woodland floor.

+3

TREE TRUNKS AND BRANCHES

CRACKS IN THE bark of trees provide a hiding place
many species of insect. Some burrow into the wood
and live completely concealed from predators. Man
insects also live and feed among the different plant
that grows on tree trunks and branches.

BARK INSECTS
Insects which live on bark
are usually camouflaged,
such as barklice, which
feed on tiny fungi and
algae. Another bark insect,
the snakefly, is a predator.
When it hunts, it looks
like a tiny snake about to
strike, holding its head
high looking for prey.

+4

SNAKEFLY

+2.7

BARKLOUSE
Mesopsocus

BARKLOUSE
Loensia fasciata

Giant wood
wasp larvae feed
on wood.

WOOD WASP
This female giant wood wasp has a long,
stout egg-laying tube, or ovipositor,
which looks like a fearsome
sting. It lays eggs deep inside
the soft wood of dead or
dying trees.

Head

Antenna

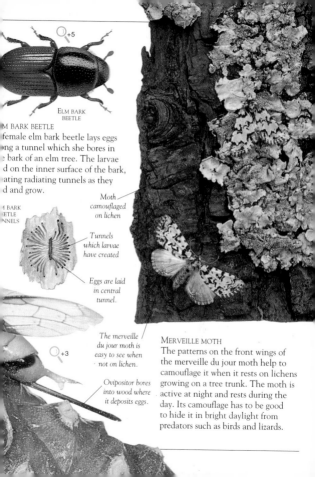

ELM BARK BEETLE

ELM BARK
BEETLE

+5

ELM BARK BEETLE
[fe]male elm bark beetle lays eggs
[alo]ng a tunnel which she bores in
[th]e bark of an elm tree. The larvae
[fee]d on the inner surface of the bark,
[cre]ating radiating tunnels as they
[fee]d and grow.

ELM BARK
BEETLE
TUNNELS

*Moth
camouflaged
on lichen*

*Tunnels
which larvae
have created*

*Eggs are laid
in central
tunnel.*

*The merveille
du jour moth is
easy to see when
not on lichen.*

+3

*Ovipositor bores
into wood where
it deposits eggs.*

MERVEILLE MOTH
The patterns on the front wings of
the merveille du jour moth help to
camouflage it when it rests on lichens
growing on a tree trunk. The moth is
active at night and rests during the
day. Its camouflage has to be good
to hide it in bright daylight from
predators such as birds and lizards.

GROUND LEVEL

THE WOODLAND floor does not get much sunlight, so few plants grow there. Most insects at ground level feed on plant and animal debris falling from the canopy, or, if they are carnivorous, eat other insects.

ANT NEST
The wood ant is a voracious predator. Colonies build huge ne[...] of plant debris, with a network of tunnels bel[...] ground providing a hom[...] for thousands of ants.

WOOD CRICKET
Most crickets are nocturnal (active at night). But the wood cricket is active on sunny days when it can be heard chirping loudly. It is unable to fly because of its short wings.

Strong jaws bite into prey.

WOOD ANT
Wood ants forage out from their nest for hundreds of yards, making distinct paths on the woodland floor. They catch huge numbers of insects and bring them to the nest in pieces as food for their young.

Ant can squirt poison from abdomen.

+8

WHITE ADMIRALS
On sunny days, white admiral butterflies can be spotted near the ground feeding on the nectar of bramble flowers. They can often be seen in the morning sipping water from puddles. They spend much of their time in the tree canopy, basking in the sunshine.

UPPERSIDE OF WHITE ADMIRAL

UNDERSIDE OF WHITE ADMIRAL

Antenna

Only male stag beetles have enlarged jaws.

...T GROUND BEETLE
beetle can run fast long legs, catching insects among the tter. It hunts mainly ht and grips its prey powerful jaws.

...BEETLE
arvae of stag beetles spend about years feeding on rotting wood a dead tree. These handsome es are now becoming rare se dead wood is often d away and burned.

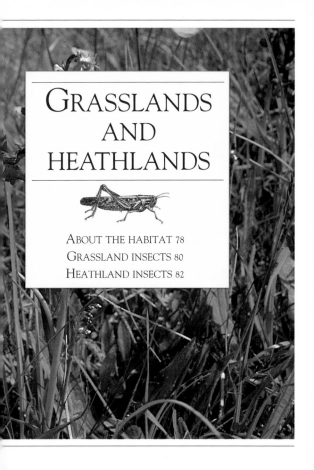

GRASSLANDS
AND
HEATHLANDS

ABOUT THE HABITAT 78
GRASSLAND INSECTS 80
HEATHLAND INSECTS 82

ABOUT THE HABITA

GRASSLANDS AND HEATHLANDS
have no protective tree canopy,
which means they change quick
with the weather – from hot and
dry to windy, cold, or wet. Thes
habitats are less complex than
forest or woodland. They provid
fewer dwelling places for inse
since there is little wood to
burrow into and hardly any
litter to dwell in.

*This grass
is called
cocks-foot.*

FIELD
CHAFER

+1.2

FOOD SOURCE
Plant roots are an
important food for
insects in these
habitats. Field
chafer larvae eat
roots, while the
adults fly from
plant to plant
seeking a mate.

SPRINGTAILS
Cultivated grass fields, such as sp
fields, support few insect species.
they do contain vast numbers of
insects called springtails. An area
size of a tennis court might be ho
up to three hundred million sprin

RD RAGWORT
d called the
d ragwort is a
on invader of
cted pasture in
e. The cinnabar
lays its eggs on
eed, and its
illars eat
ves.

CINNABAR
MOTH

⌕ _.8

GRASSLAND AND
HEATHLAND FACTS

• The grasslands of
Argentina are called
Pampas, or "plains" in
the language of the
native people.

• Prairies of the US
have tall grasses.

• Steppes (prairielike
land) of Siberia have
short grasses.

moth has
g coloration
se it tastes
leasant.

An Oxford
ragwort is often
stripped of its leaves
by feeding caterpillars.

N PLANT LIFE
al grassland and
land have a huge
y of grasses
owering
. These rich
ts buzz with
life

r
s.

CRANESBILL

EXTINCT BUTTERFLY
The English large copper
butterfly was once common
in fenland but is now
extinct. This is a result of
intensive land development
for agriculture, which
destroyed the butterfly's
special food plant.

GRASSLAND INSECTS

MOST INSECT species cannot survive in cultivated g
lands, such as garden lawns, since they usually cont
only one type of grass. Also, weedkillers and other
chemicals harm many insects. But natural grasslan
with their variety of plants, support thousands of in
species that have adapted to this open, windy habit

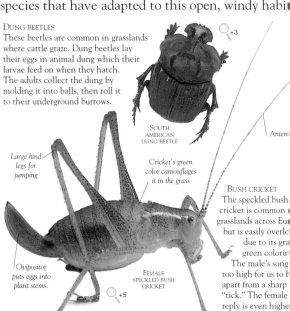

DUNG BEETLES
These beetles are common in grasslands
where cattle graze. Dung beetles lay
their eggs in animal dung which their
larvae feed on when they hatch.
The adults collect the dung by
molding it into balls, then roll it
to their underground burrows.

Q +3

SOUTH
AMERICAN
DUNG BEETLE

Anten

Large hind
legs for
jumping

Cricket's green
color camouflages
it in the grass

BUSH CRICKET
The speckled bush
cricket is common i
grasslands across Eu
but is easily overlo
due to its gra
green colorir
The male's song
too high for us to h
apart from a sharp
"tick." The female
reply is even highe

Ovipositor
puts eggs into
plant stems.

FEMALE
SPECKLED BUSH
CRICKET

Q +5

80

ATER
are so many ants in
asslands of South
ica and Africa
pecialized
ating
nals have
ed. They have
ful claws to break open ant
and long sticky tongues to
t the ants.

ANTEATER

Q −.8

LARGE BLUE BUTTERFLY
This butterfly lays its eggs
on the wild thyme plant,
and the newly hatched
caterpillars feed on thyme
flowers. The caterpillars
attract red ants with a
special milk. The ants are
deceived into carrying the
caterpillars into their nest,
where the caterpillars eat
the ant eggs and larva.

Q +1.3

LED WHITE BUTTERFLY
utterfly can be found in a
y of grassland habitats, including
areas inside woodland. Marbled
s often gather in groups to
n the early morning and
evening sunshine.

Ragwort
flowers

Mating
soldier beetles

Q −.3

ER BEETLES
insects feed on one particular
r, while others, such as
r beetles, eat pollen from
s flowers. These feeding
re also good places for
s to find a mate.

HEATHLAND INSECTS

MANY BURROWING insects live in heathl
since the soil is loose and easy to dig
into. Heathland occurs in parts of th
world with a climate of rainy winte
and warm, dry summers. It has a ri
mixture of plants, and the soil,
which is often sandy, warn
up quickly in the sunshir

*Butterfly
is hard to
spot in the
grass.*

GRAYLING BUTTERFLY
The tops of the wings of
grayling butterfly are bri
colored, while their und
is mottled gray for camo
on the ground. When re
it folds back its wings ar
sometimes leans toward
sun so it casts no shadov

COMMON
YELLOW
DUNG FLY

Q +4

*Dung flies eat
other insects,
which they kill
with piercing
mouthparts.*

DUNG FLY
Wherever cattle are grazing, insects v
found breeding in the cattle's nutritic
dung. Dung flies lay their eggs on fres
deposited cow pats. The maggots hate
few hours later and start eating the d

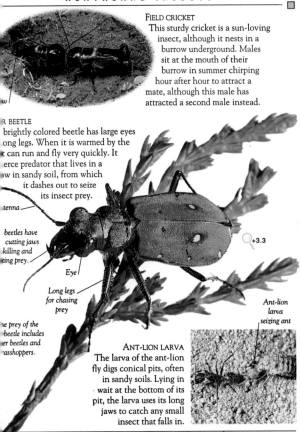

FIELD CRICKET
This sturdy cricket is a sun-loving insect, although it nests in a burrow underground. Males sit at the mouth of their burrow in summer chirping hour after hour to attract a mate, although this male has attracted a second male instead.

R BEETLE
brightly colored beetle has large eyes
ong legs. When it is warmed by the
can run and fly very quickly. It
rce predator that lives in a
w in sandy soil, from which
it dashes out to seize
its insect prey.

tenna

beetles have
cutting jaws
killing and
ting prey.

Eye

Long legs
for chasing
prey

+3.3

e prey of the
beetle includes
er beetles and
rasshoppers.

Ant-lion
larva
seizing ant

ANT-LION LARVA
The larva of the ant-lion fly digs conical pits, often in sandy soils. Lying in wait at the bottom of its pit, the larva uses its long jaws to catch any small insect that falls in.

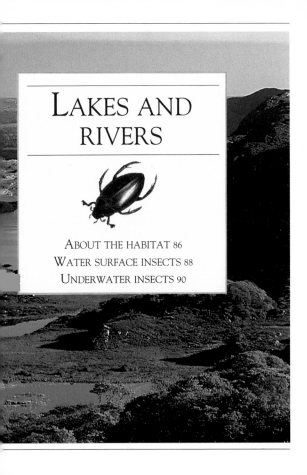

LAKES AND RIVERS

ABOUT THE HABITAT 86

WATER SURFACE INSECTS 88

UNDERWATER INSECTS 90

ABOUT THE HABITAT

INSECTS CAN be found in all sorts
of freshwater habitats: lakes,
fast-flowing streams, ponds,
puddles, damp moss, and wet
leaf litter. These insects have
many adaptations for surviving
in their watery homes.

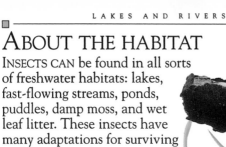

This case is ~
of a mixtur~
leaves an~
stones.

+3

*The stony case is
held together by silk
woven by the larva.*

Head

Legs hold
onto plant.

*Flowers attract
nectar-eating
insects.*

*The flat leaves have
a water-repellent waxy
covering so they don't
get waterlogged.*

CADDIS FLY LAR~
Insects are in danger of
swept away in fast-fl
water. Cac
larvae build a case around their b~
protection, and often the cases are
of heavy stone to weigh the larvae

FRINGED WATERLILY
The tangled stems of the fringed
waterlily are a good h~
place for pond insect
Dragonflies also find
leaves and stems a safe plac~
which to lay their eggs.

Leg — *Breathing tube*

Head of caddis fly larva

Case made of leaves

○ +2

GILLS
A caddis fly larva has gills for taking oxygen from the water. The larva undulates its body to create a flow of oxygen-rich water over its gills inside the case.

WATER SCORPION
The water scorpion has a breathing tube on its rear end so it can breathe the outside air while it is underwater. Insects with breathing tubes can survive in warm ponds or polluted waters that are low in oxygen.

SPRINGTAILS
In corners of ponds sheltered from the wind, swarms of springtails sometimes gather on the surface of the water. They feed on organic debris that has blown into the pond.

FAST STREAMS
Insects that live in fast-flowing streams have streamlined bodies and strong claws to help them cling to stones. The water that passes over their gills is always rich in oxygen, but low temperatures mean that larvae develop more slowly than they would in a shallow, sun-warmed pond.

LAKES AND RIVERS FACTS

• Fish populations depend on plenty of insects as food.

• Dragonfly larvae are considered a delicacy in New Guinea.

• Swarms of nonbiting midges are sometimes so dense over African lakes that fishermen have been suffocated.

WATER SURFACE INSECTS

A WATER SURFACE behaves like a skin due to a force called surface tension. This force enables certain insects to walk on the "skin," and others to hang just beneath it. Many of these insects are predators, and much of their food comes from the constant supply flying insects which have fallen into the water.

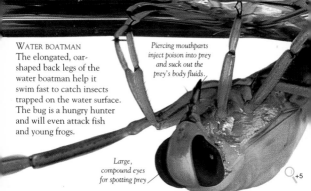

⊘+6

WHIRLIGIG
The whirligig beetle swims around and around very fast on the water surface. It hunts insects trapped on the surface tension. The whirligig's eyes are divided into two halves, allowing it to see both above and below the water surface at the same time.

WATER BOATMAN
The elongated, oar-shaped back legs of the water boatman help it swim fast to catch insects trapped on the water surface. The bug is a hungry hunter and will even attack fish and young frogs.

Piercing mouthparts inject poison into prey and suck out the prey's body fluids.

Large, compound eyes for spotting prey

⊘+5

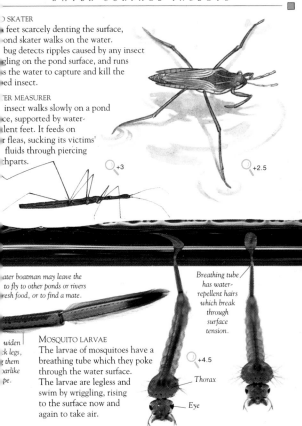

O SKATER

feet scarcely denting the surface,
ond skater walks on the water.
bug detects ripples caused by any insect
gling on the pond surface, and runs
s the water to capture and kill the
ed insect.

ER MEASURER

insect walks slowly on a pond
ce, supported by water-
lent feet. It feeds on
fleas, sucking its victims'
fluids through piercing
chparts.

Q +3

Q +2.5

ater boatman may leave the
to fly to other ponds or rivers
resh food, or to find a mate.

*Breathing tube
has water-
repellent hairs
which break
through
surface
tension.*

widen
k legs,
them
arlike
pe.

MOSQUITO LARVAE
The larvae of mosquitoes have a
breathing tube which they poke
through the water surface.
The larvae are legless and
swim by wriggling, rising
to the surface now and
again to take air.

Q +4.5

Thorax

Eye

8 9

UNDERWATER INSECTS

MANY OF THE insects that live underwater are carnivorous, either hunting their prey or scavenging. Some of these insects are fierce, sometimes killing prey larger than themselves.

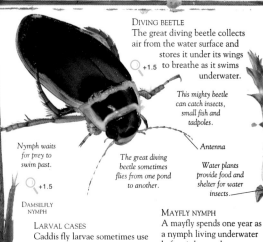

DIVING BEETLE
The great diving beetle collects air from the water surface and stores it under its wings to breathe as it swims underwater.

+1.5

This mighty beetle can catch insects, small fish and tadpoles.

Nymph waits for prey to swim past.

+1.5

DAMSELFLY NYMPH

The great diving beetle sometimes flies from one pond to another.

Antenna

Water plants provide food and shelter for water insects.

LARVAL CASES
Caddis fly larvae sometimes use pieces of plant to make their protective cases. This body armor also acts as camouflage.

Pieces of plant

MAYFLY NYMPH
A mayfly spends one year as a nymph living underwater before it leaves the water to become an adult. The nymph breathes through gills along the side of its abdomen.

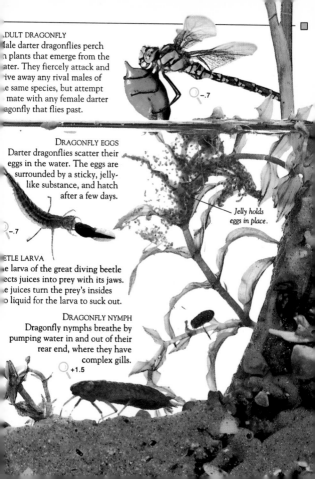

ADULT DRAGONFLY
Male darter dragonflies perch on plants that emerge from the water. They fiercely attack and drive away any rival males of the same species, but attempt to mate with any female darter dragonfly that flies past.

−.7

DRAGONFLY EGGS
Darter dragonflies scatter their eggs in the water. The eggs are surrounded by a sticky, jelly-like substance, and hatch after a few days.

Jelly holds eggs in place.

BEETLE LARVA
The larva of the great diving beetle injects juices into prey with its jaws. The juices turn the prey's insides into liquid for the larva to suck out.

−.7

DRAGONFLY NYMPH
Dragonfly nymphs breathe by pumping water in and out of their rear end, where they have complex gills.

+1.5

TROPICAL
FOREST

ABOUT THE HABITAT 94

IN THE CANOPY 96

NESTS IN THE CANOPY 98

BRILLIANT BUTTERFLIES 100

TROPICAL BUTTERFLIES 102

HORNED BEETLES 104

THE LARGEST INSECTS 106

STICK AND LEAF INSECTS 108

ARMIES ON THE GROUND 110

ABOUT THE HABITA

INSECTS THRIVE in the humid he
and flourishing plant life of trop
forests. These forests have a
complex structure that provides
many habitats for insects. Trees
vary in shape and size; vines and
dead branches are everywhere, a
thick leaf litter covers the groun

ORCHID

ORCHIDS

Tropical forests contain a
spectacular variety of plants
– there are about 25,000
species of orchid alone. It
is quite dark beneath
the forest canopy and
orchids are strongly scented
to help insects find them.

EPIPHYTES

Many plants grow o
trunks and branche
trees where birds l
wiped seeds from
beaks. These tree-
dwelling plants, ca
epiphytes, provide e
habitats for insects.

INSECT PREDATORS

A tropical forest is a rich habitat
for birds as well as insects.
Tropical birds feed on countless
insects each day. This high rate
of predation is a major reason for
the evolution of camouflage and
mimicry in tropical insects.

FRUITY NOURISHMENT

Some tropical
butterflies live for
several months. An
important source of
fuel for their continued
activity is rotting fruit
and dung on the forest
floor. This gives them
not only sugars for
energy, but also amino
acids and vitamins
needed for survival.

Until recently, this insect was known only from dull brown museum specimens.

Blue face

Red eye

TROPICAL FORESTS

Bright colors are typical of tropical forests, and they can be seen in both the plant and animal life. This Central American grasshopper looks as if it would be easy to spot with its multicolored body, but it is camouflaged among the shining leaves of the forest trees.

The bright colors of this grasshopper surprised even entomologists.

Bright green abdomen

+2

The grasshopper's colors fade when it dies.

TROPICAL FOREST FACTS

• Tropical forests cover about five percent of the Earth's land surface.

• They contain over half of all living species.

• Around 1,200 species of butterfly have been recorded in one forest in southern Peru.

• Over half the world's rainforest has been cut since 1945.

IN THE CANOPY

THERE IS WARMTH, light, and plenty of food to eat i
the canopy of tropical trees. The canopy
provides living space for thousands of ins
species. In one day 3,000 different speci
were collected from a single tree
in a forest in Borneo.

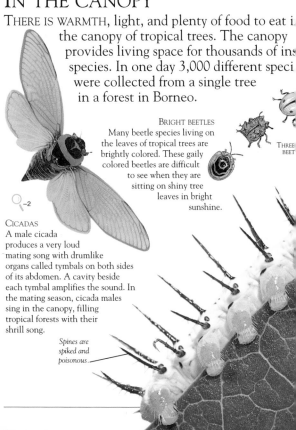

BRIGHT BEETLES
Many beetle species living on
the leaves of tropical trees are
brightly colored. These gaily
colored beetles are difficult
to see when they are
sitting on shiny tree
leaves in bright
sunshine.

THREE
BEET

CICADAS
A male cicada
produces a very loud
mating song with drumlike
organs called tymbals on both sides
of its abdomen. A cavity beside
each tymbal amplifies the sound. In
the mating season, cicada males
sing in the canopy, filling
tropical forests with their
shrill song.

*Spines are
spiked and
poisonous.*

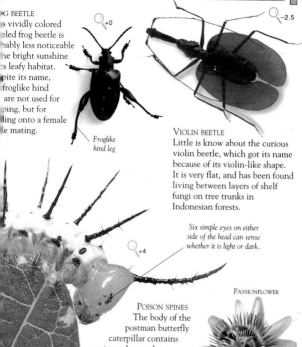

G BEETLE

s vividly colored
eled frog beetle is
ably less noticeable
he bright sunshine
s leafy habitat.
pite its name,
froglike hind
are not used for
ping, but for
ling onto a female
e mating.

*Froglike
hind leg*

Q +0

Q −2.5

VIOLIN BEETLE

Little is know about the curious
violin beetle, which got its name
because of its violin-like shape.
It is very flat, and has been found
living between layers of shelf
fungi on tree trunks in
Indonesian forests.

*Six simple eyes on either
side of the head can sense
whether it is light or dark.*

Q +4

PASSIONFLOWER

POISON SPINES

The body of the
postman butterfly
caterpillar contains
poisons. It gets the
poisons from chemicals
in the leaves of the
passionflower vines
that it eats. The
prickly spines remind
birds to avoid it.

NESTS IN THE CANOPY

WITH SO MANY insects feeding in the
forest canopy, it is not surprising that
the insect-eating ants and wasps
build their nests there. But these
ants and wasps are in turn hunted
by mammals and lizards, so their
nests must give protection.

Nest
of pa
ma

GREEN WEAVER ANTS

Each green weaver ant colony has several nests
made of leaves. To make a nest, the ants join
forces to pull leaves together and sew the edges.
They sew using silk which the larvae produce
when they are squeezed by the adult ants. These
carnivorous ants hunt through the tree canopy,
catching other insects and carrying the
prey in pieces back to
the ants' nests.

WASP NESTS

Each wasp species makes a
different type of nest. This
from South America has b
cut in half to reveal the "f
which house the larvae. T
one small opening at the b
where the wasps defend th
from invading ants.

*Ants pulling
leaves together.*

*This nest hangs
from a branch
of a tree.*

*There may be
half a million ants
in one weaver
ant colony.*

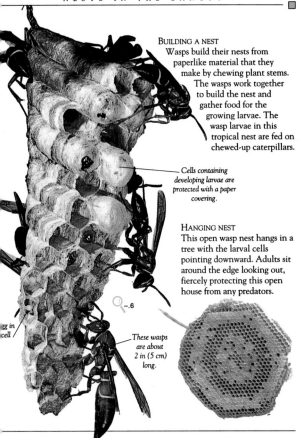

BUILDING A NEST

Wasps build their nests from paperlike material that they make by chewing plant stems. The wasps work together to build the nest and gather food for the growing larvae. The wasp larvae in this tropical nest are fed on chewed-up caterpillars.

Cells containing developing larvae are protected with a paper covering.

HANGING NEST

This open wasp nest hangs in a tree with the larval cells pointing downward. Adults sit around the edge looking out, fiercely protecting this open house from any predators.

gg in cell

These wasps are about 2 in (5 cm) long.

BRILLIANT BUTTERFLIES

MANY TROPICAL butterflies are large and brilliantly colored, which ought to make them easy for predators to catch them. But they fly rapidly and erratically, flash their bright colors in the sun, and then seem to disappear, darting into the deep shade of the forest.

BLUE MORPHO
The iridescent blue of South American morpho butterflies is so vivid it can be seen from a great distance. But its underwings are a muddy brown camouflage when feeding on the ground.

Q -.3

SOUTHEAST ASIAN MOTH
The vivid colors of this southeast Asian moth shows that some day-flying moths can be as colorful as butterflies. The bright colors warn predators that this moth is poisonous.

Q +2

NERO BUTTERFLY
The bright yellow Nero butterfly drinks from streams and puddles near mammal dung. This habit is common in butterflies of tropical forests, and supplies them with nutrients that are not available in flowers.

+2

re
d

POSTMAN BUTTERFLY
Brightly colored and slow-flying, the postman butterfly is poisonous to predators, who quickly learn to avoid them. Groups of postman butterflies often sleep together on branches.

FEMALE BIRDWING BUTTERFLY

-3.2

BIRDWING BUTTERFLIES
The males of southeast Asian birdwing butterflies differ in size, color, and behavior from the females. The brightly colored males sometimes fly near the ground, but the larger brownish females remain in the treetops.

MALE BIRDWING BUTTERFLY

3

TROPICAL BUTTERFLIE

THOUSANDS OF butterfly species live
tropical forests. Each butterfly has
recognize members of its own spe
among all the others in order to n
They find each other by sight –
butterflies have a good sense of co
and by smell.

Tail brush

USING SCENTS
Striped blue crow butterfly
males have a yellow brush
at the end of their
abdomen. When a male
has found a female, he uses
his brush to dust scented
scales on her. The arousing
scent encourages the
female to mate with him.

DETECTING SCENTS
The complex nature of a
silkmoth antenna can be
seen when viewed at high
magnification. It is divided
into segments, and each
segment has two branches.
The branches increase the
antenna's surface area,
making it more sensitive.

_Branches on
each segment_

_Scent chemi
stimulate ner
the antenn_

SITTING TOGETHER
At sunny spots in the forest,
butterflies gather at muddy puddles to
drink water and salts. Butterflies of the
same species usually sit together, so that
white-colored species form one group,
blue another, and so on.

Postman butterflies and small postman butterflies are two different species. But they share the same wing patterns in different parts of South America.

POSTMAN BUTTERFLY
FROM SOUTHERN ECUADOR

SMALL POSTMAN BUTTERFLY
FROM SOUTHERN ECUADOR

SMALL POSTMAN BUTTERFLY
FROM SOUTHERN BRAZIL

POSTMAN BUTTERFLY
FROM SOUTHERN BRAZIL

SMALL POSTMAN BUTTERFLY
FROM WESTERN BRAZIL

POSTMAN BUTTERFLY
FROM WESTERN BRAZIL

COPYING PATTERNS

Sometimes two or more different species of poisonous butterfly share the same wing pattern. This kind of mimicry means that the different species protect each other. Birds only need to learn that one species is poisonous to avoid the other.

HORNED BEETLES

WITH SO MANY millions of insect in tropical forests, individuals m sometimes compete for the best living space in which to mate and lay eggs. Horned beetles have hor which they use as weapons battle. A male may lock horr with other males to claim a go territory, and then attract females to him.

Jaws have spines running along them.

Darwin's beetle is from Brazil.

Antenna

Spiny front leg

Q –.5

DARWIN'S BEETLE
This beetle probably uses its long jaws to drive away rival males. Darwin's beetle is supposed to have bitten Charles Darwin, the famous naturalist, when he was in Brazil.

The rhinoceros beetle can lift 850 times its own weight.

The beetle may use its horns to lift a rival out of the way.

RHINOCEROS B
Within the same sp rhinoceros beetle male their horns can vary gr in size. Sometimes, whe biggest male fighting, one o smalles sneakely mate the female o of the fig n

This male rhinoceros beetle is 3½ in (9 cm) long.

Clawed feet

Q –.5

Q—.4

*le stretches
*s antennae
* pick up
*ormation
t its rival.

DUNG BEETLE
Horns are not only
used for fighting. Dung
beetles roll fresh dung
into balls using spade-
shaped horns. They
then bury the balls
and the females lay
an egg on each one.

TING STAGS
*tle fights usually involve
*atening behavior and
*stling. These two
*e stag beetles are
*g each other up
re fighting.

LIFTING HORNS
One male stag beetle has gotten
the better of its opponent. Beetle
fights rarely involve killing, but if
one male lifts another and drops
it from a branch the victim
might be stunned and
no longer pose a
threat.

*Like most males in the
animal kingdom, male
beetles usually fight over
erritory, females, or food.*

Q+1.5

*The "horns" of
stag beetles are
actually
enlarged jaws.*

*Beetle grips
branch with
claws on its feet.*

THE LARGEST INSECTS

SOME OF THE largest insects live in tropical forests, where the warm temperatures and abundance of food allow them to grow quickly. But insects cannot grow very large, since their simple breathing system could not cope with a large body. Also, big insects would be easy prey for birds and mammals.

ATLAS MOTH
With a wingspar 6 in (15 cm), the at moth has the largest wi area of all insects. Silvery p on each wing shine like mirro

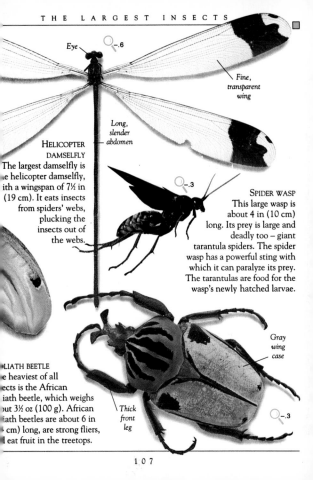

Eye

○−.6

Fine,
transparent
wing

Long,
slender
abdomen

**HELICOPTER
DAMSELFLY**
The largest damselfly is
he helicopter damselfly,
ith a wingspan of 7½ in
(19 cm). It eats insects
from spiders' webs,
plucking the
insects out of
the webs.

○−.3

SPIDER WASP
This large wasp is
about 4 in (10 cm)
long. Its prey is large and
deadly too – giant
tarantula spiders. The spider
wasp has a powerful sting with
which it can paralyze its prey.
The tarantulas are food for the
wasp's newly hatched larvae.

Gray
wing
case

LIATH BEETLE
e heaviest of all
ects is the African
iath beetle, which weighs
ut 3½ oz (100 g). African
iath beetles are about 6 in
cm) long, are strong fliers,
l eat fruit in the treetops.

Thick
front
leg

○−.3

STICK AND LEAF INSECTS

A TROPICAL FOREST is alive with animals, most of
which eat insects. To survive, insects adopt many
strategies. Stick and leaf insects hide from predators
by keeping still and resembling their background
of leaves and sticks.

STICK INSECTS
Some stick insects are
slender, brown, or green,
just like the twigs and
leaf stalks they sit on.
Other species are
shorter and fatter,
with spines and other
projections. These
often look like curled
dead leaves.

*Winged male of
Macleay's spectre*

*Wingless female of
Macleay's spectre*

*Indian stick
insect*

*Spiny
green
nymph*

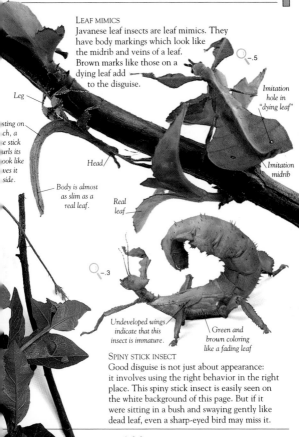

LEAF MIMICS
Javanese leaf insects are leaf mimics. They
have body markings which look like
the midrib and veins of a leaf.
Brown marks like those on a
dying leaf add
to the disguise.

-.5

Imitation
hole in
"dying leaf"

Leg

sting on
ch, a
e stick
urls its
ook like
ves it
side.

Imitation
midrib

Head

Body is almost
as slim as a
real leaf.

Real
leaf

-.3

Undeveloped wings
indicate that this
insect is immature.

Green and
brown coloring
like a fading leaf

SPINY STICK INSECT
Good disguise is not just about appearance:
it involves using the right behavior in the right
place. This spiny stick insect is easily seen on
the white background of this page. But if it
were sitting in a bush and swaying gently like
dead leaf, even a sharp-eyed bird may miss it.

ARMIES ON THE GROUND

ANTS ARE THE dominant creatures of tropical forest. They live in colonies made up of any number from 20 individuals to many thousands. Ants are mostly carnivorous. Some species make slaves of other ant species by invading their nest and killing their que

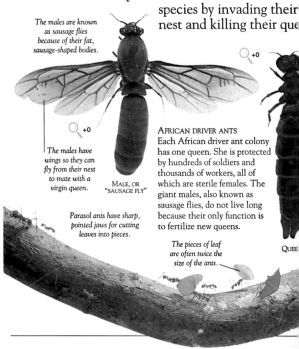

The males are known as sausage flies because of their fat, sausage-shaped bodies.

Q +0

The males have wings so they can fly from their nest to mate with a virgin queen.

MALE, OR "SAUSAGE FLY"

Parasol ants have sharp, pointed jaws for cutting leaves into pieces.

AFRICAN DRIVER ANTS
Each African driver ant colony has one queen. She is protected by hundreds of soldiers and thousands of workers, all of which are sterile females. The giant males, also known as sausage flies, do not live long because their only function is to fertilize new queens.

The pieces of leaf are often twice the size of the ants.

QUE

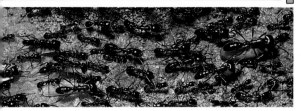

...ER ANTS MARCHING

...e ants get their name from the way a colony
...s through an area catching all the insects it
...nd. They move their nests from place to
...regularly, unlike most ants which have a
...anent nest and territory.

*Beetle pupae
are among
the prey of
driver ants.*

...RYING PREY

...in a column collaborate to cut
...insects they have caught into
...er pieces. This is so they can carry
...food back to the nest. Smaller
...can be carried whole.

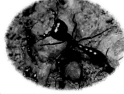

ATTENTIVE SOLDIER
Driver ant soldiers have very large
jaws. Often they can be seen
standing beside a marching column
of ants with their jaws wide open,
waiting to attack intruders
such as parasitic flies.

*Ant returning
for more leaves*

PARASOL ANTS
These South American ants are
not carnivorous. They feed on fungus which
they cultivate in huge underground nests. The fungus is
grown on pieces of leaf which the ants bring to the nest.

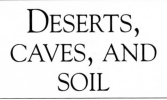

DESERTS, CAVES, AND SOIL

ABOUT THE HABITAT 114
DESERT INSECTS 116
CAVE INSECTS 118
SOIL INSECTS 120

ABOUT THE HABITAT

SOME INSECTS flourish in habitats where it is difficul
for living things to survive. Desert habitats, for
example, lack water and have very high temperatur
Caves are dark and lack plant life for food. Life in s
makes communication, by both
scent and sight, difficult
for insects.

*Tiger beetle
larva has hooks
on body to help it
climb upward.*

HIDING IN SOIL

Life in the soil is only a pas
phase for some insect speci
This tiger beetle larva hide
underground by day. At ni
waits in its vertical tunnel
its jaws projecting at the g
surface, and snatches pass
insects to devour in its b

CAVE DWELLER

This cockroach lives all
life in the dark. Like ot
cave creatures, it feeds
debris from the outsid
world. Bat dung, dead
animals, and pieces
plants washed into t
cave provide the
cockroach with its
nourishment.

[DES]ERT BEETLE

[The] lack of water in deserts forces insects to [find] ingenious ways of obtaining moisture. This [darkling] beetle lives in the Namib Desert, [where] sea winds bring mists each night. The [beetle] holds its abdomen high to catch the [moi]sture, which then runs down into its mouth.

DESERT HEAT

The hot and dry days in deserts can lead to rapid water loss and death for animals. Most living creatures hide under stones or in the sand to avoid drying out. These animals are active at night when it is much cooler.

[DE]SERT FACTS

[T]he Sahara Desert is [spr]eading at a rate of [3 m]iles (5 km) per year.

[I]n deserts the [te]mperature may range [fro]m 90°F (30°C) in [th]e day to below 32°F [(0°]C) at night.

[C]aves are a nearly [co]nstant temperature [th]roughout the year.

[2]0% of the Earth's [lan]d surface [is d]esert.

CACTUS FLOWER

DESERT PLANTS

Rain may not fall in a desert for months, or even years. Most desert plants store water so they can survive, and some desert animals rely on these plants for food. But many animals, including some insects, migrate in search of rain and the plant growth it produces.

DESERT INSECTS

HOT, DRY DESERTS are dangerous places in which to
live. Animals often die from sunstroke and dehydra
(drying out). To prevent this, insects avoid the sun
staying in the shade or burrowing in the sand. Som
insects have special methods of collecting water. M
feed only at night, because the surface of the sand i
too hot for them to walk on during the day.

–.7

NAMIB DESERT BEETLE
Long legs keep the body of the Namib desert
beetle off the hot sand. The larvae live in the
sand, scavenging on detritus (organic debris),
and complete development in about six
months. The adults live for several years.

Anten

DESERT LOCUSTS
Adult desert locusts fly in swarms
to find fresh food. When there
is enough food they breed
rapidly, and huge groups of
wingless nymphs hop
across the desert sand.

*Grasses and
other plants form
the diet of desert
locusts.*

*Desert locusts
get water from
plant food.*

TWO D
LOCUST N

+2

CRICKET
rge feet of
sert cricket
t to dig
ly in the sand. It
ry itself in a few
s, either to hide
redators or to
from
ense
f the midday sun.
gtips are coiled
ect them
underground.

–.5

End of
wings
coiled up

Large feet

Long
antenna

back
r long
ps

This hard
collar protects
the thorax.

Wing
buds

HONEYPOT ANTS
Honeypot ants are living water
stores. During the rainy season,
certain worker ants in a colony
are fed with water and nectar
until their abdomens are full
and swollen. In the dry season
the other ants feed from them
until the rainy season returns.

JEWEL WASP
These shiny green wasps
catch other insects, such as
cockroaches, for their young
to eat. Adult jewel wasps are
vegetarians, drinking nectar
from desert flowers. +1.2

CAVE INSECTS

ALL LIFE DEPENDS on the sun's energy. Plants change sunlight into food by a process called photosynthesis. In dark, sunless caves, nothing grows, and cave dwelling insects must find food from outside. This food is sometimes washed in on floods, or dropped by bats and birds.

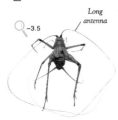

Long antenna

−3.5

AFRICAN CRICKET
Some insects have developed very long antennae to make up for lack of vision in dark caves. This African cricket has the longest antennae for its body size of any insect.

Long back legs for jumping out of danger

FEMALE AFRICAN CAVE CRICKET

Two sensitive spines, called cerci, can detect enemies approaching from behind.

Cricket uses its ovipositor (egg-laying tube) to lay eggs in soil.

+2.5

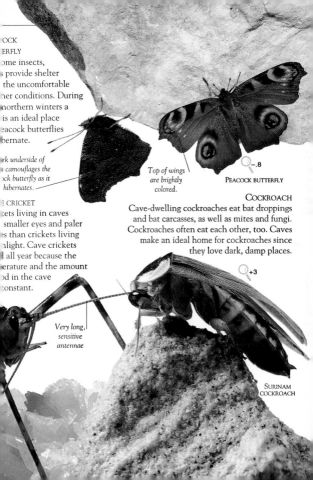

OCK
ERFLY

ome insects,
provide shelter
the uncomfortable
her conditions. During
northern winters a
is an ideal place
eacock butterflies
bernate.

rk underside of
camouflages the
ock butterfly as it
hibernates.

Top of wings
are brightly
colored.

Q —.8

PEACOCK BUTTERFLY

COCKROACH

Cave-dwelling cockroaches eat bat droppings
and bat carcasses, as well as mites and fungi.
Cockroaches often eat each other, too. Caves
make an ideal home for cockroaches since
they love dark, damp places.

Q +3

E CRICKET

ets living in caves
smaller eyes and paler
es than crickets living
light. Cave crickets
all year because the
erature and the amount
d in the cave
onstant.

Very long,
sensitive
antennae

SURINAM
COCKROACH

SOIL INSECTS

WHEN PLANTS and animals die, their remains usuall
get absorbed into the soil. Insects that live in soil a
among the most important creatures on Earth beca
they help to recycle these remains, releasing their
nutrients and so helping new crops and forests to
grow. Soil insects are also an
important food for many
mammals and birds.

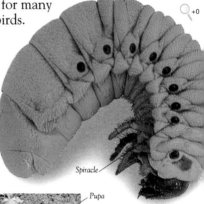

BEETLE LARVA
Roots and decaying tree
trunks provide food for
many types of insect
larva, such as this
lamellicorn beetle grub.
The grub breathes
through holes called
spiracles, which occur
along the side of its
body. Although there
is not very much air
underground, there is
enough for insects.

Spiracle

Pupa

GOOD HABITAT
Living in soil has advantages. Ir
are unlikely to dehydrate, and t
is plenty of food in plant roots a
decaying plants. This spurge ha
moth pupa has sharp plates on i
abdomen which help it climb t
surface just before the adult eme

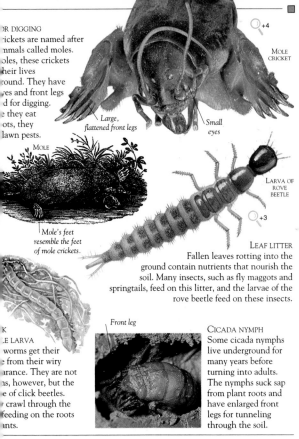

+4

MOLE
CRICKET

OR DIGGING
rickets are named after
nmals called mole-
oles, these crickets
heir lives
round. They have
yes and front legs
e for digging.
e they eat
ots, they
lawn pests.

*Large,
flattened front legs*

*Small
eyes*

MOLE

*Mole's feet
resemble the feet
of mole crickets.*

LARVA OF
ROVE BEETLE

+3

LEAF LITTER

Fallen leaves rotting into the
ground contain nutrients that nourish the
soil. Many insects, such as fly maggots and
springtails, feed on this litter, and the larvae of the
rove beetle feed on these insects.

K
LE LARVA
worms get their
e from their wiry
arance. They are not
ns, however, but the
e of click beetles.
crawl through the
eeding on the roots
nts.

Front leg

CICADA NYMPH

Some cicada nymphs
live underground for
many years before
turning into adults.
The nymphs suck sap
from plant roots and
have enlarged front
legs for tunneling
through the soil.

TOWNS AND GARDENS

ABOUT THE HABITAT 124
HOUSEHOLD INSECTS 126
GARDEN INSECTS 128
FRIENDS AND FOES 130
BEES AND POLLINATION 132

ABOUT THE HABITAT

SINCE INSECTS HAVE managed to make homes for themselves in practically every natural habitat, it is surprising that they have turned human habitats in their homes, too. Insects live in our houses, feeding our furniture, clothes, foodstores, and garbage dump Our gardens and farms are also teeming with insect li nourished by the abundance of flower fruits and vegetables

Colorado beetle

⊖ –1.4

POTATO PESTS
When potatoes were brought to Europe from South America, the Colorado beetle came with them. This insect eats potato plant leaves, and can cause great damage to crops.

Leaves of potato plant

Potato

CABBAGE EATERS
Cabbage white butterflies lay eggs on cabbage plants so the larvae can eat the leaves. Farms provide acres o cabbages, and the butterflies become pests since they br at an unnaturally rate because of the abundance of food

WASPS IN OUR HOMES

The roofs of our houses keep us warm and dry, but they also provide ideal conditions for wasps' nests. Wasps are useful to us in summer since they catch our garden insect pests to feed to their young.

Nest hangs from rafters.

INFESTATIONS

uch as cockroaches are
to make use of any food
we waste. Uncovered or
food in kitchens allows
nsects to thrive, and can
an infestation that
to eliminate.

GREENHOUSES

In temperate countries, tropical insects often thrive in greenhouses, which reproduce tropical conditions. Butterfly farms use this principle to breed exotic insects for us to look at and enjoy.

The monarch butterfly is bred on butterfly farms.

WNS AND DENS FACTS

ore than 1,800
ct species were
d in a typical
ish garden.

wer than one
ent of cockroach
ies are considered
e pests.

acock butterflies
spend the winter
rden sheds.

HOUSEHOLD INSECTS

SINCE PREHISTORIC times, insects have lived in hu
homes, attracted by warmth, shelter, and food. Th
insects eat our food, our furniture, and some even
our carpets. Parasitic insects also live in our homes
feeding on the human inhabitants.

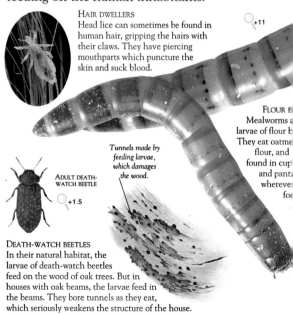

HAIR DWELLERS
Head lice can sometimes be found in
human hair, gripping the hairs with
their claws. They have piercing
mouthparts which puncture the
skin and suck blood.

+11

FLOUR E
Mealworms a
larvae of flour b
They eat oatme
flour, and
found in cup
and pant
wherever
fo

*Tunnels made by
feeding larvae,
which damages
the wood.*

ADULT DEATH-
WATCH BEETLE

+1.5

DEATH-WATCH BEETLES
In their natural habitat, the
larvae of death-watch beetles
feed on the wood of oak trees. But in
houses with oak beams, the larvae feed in
the beams. They bore tunnels as they eat,
which seriously weakens the structure of the house.

...lworm has
...mented
...ton which
...flexibility.

BED BUGS

CARPET EATERS
The larvae of ...pet beetles, called ...rmestids, eat wool. ...can be a pest since ...hey chew holes in woolen carpets.

BED BUGS
Prehistoric humans shared their caves with bats and birds, in whose nests were blood-sucking bugs. Some of these, including bed bugs, developed a taste for human blood, and have been with us ever since.

...N OUR HOME
...lies can be found
...t households
...hout the world.
...rvae, called
...ts, feed on our
...e and food.
...houseflies
...n food we
...ncovered.
...an be harmful
...e houseflies
...iisease-
...g organisms
...ir feet.

Houseflies taste food with their feet.

+4

Spongelike mouthparts soak up food.

GARDEN INSECTS

A GARDEN IS a good place to watch and study insec
Many different insects are attracted into gardens to
feed on the flowers, vegetables, and other plants. S
predatory insects come to eat the plant-eating inse

But most garden insec
are just tourists, feedin
on flower nectar as the
pass through.

ROVE BEETLES
Rove beetles hunt at night,
scouring the garden for
insects to eat. These large
beetles are common in
compost piles, scurrying
away from the daylight
when the compost is
turned.

+2.5

GARDENER'S FRIENDS
Hoverflies hover in front of f
on hot, sunny days as they fe
nectar. They are particularly
attracted to thistle flower
Hoverfly larvae are the
gardener's friends, feed
voraciously on plant-
damaging aphids.

+3

Eye

Antenna

X-MOTH
aterpillars of
-moths can
ognized by their
erect "tail." Most
phinx-moths fly at
hovering in front of
s to gather nectar with
ong tongues.

SILVER-STRIPED SPHINX-
MOTH CATERPILLAR

"Tail"

+0

Eyespot

Caterpillar has
eyespots to frighten
off predators.

Fuchsia
flower

EN GRASSHOPPER
ommon field grasshopper is widespread in
e on short grass in sunny places, and often
a home in gardens. Like tropical locusts,
on field grasshoppers sometimes migrate in
s, but on a much smaller scale.

RED
ADMIRAL

–.3

Butterflies
often stop to
sunbathe for
a while.

FOR BUTTERFLIES
lower border of a garden is like a filling
n for passing butterflies. They feed on
r to give them energy as they search for
le mates or plants on which to lay eggs.

PEACOCK

SILVER-SPOTTED
SKIPPER

–.3

FRIENDS AND FOES

THE RELATIONSHIP between insects ar
humans is not always good. Many ins
are useful to us, although others are
pests. We destroy their habitats, and
deny other wild animals of food.
  Ecology, involving the study of the
balance between our needs and the
needs of other animals and plants
helps us to understand this confl

*Aphids drink
the rose's sap. This
may kill the rose,
because the sap
is like the
plant's blood.*

APHIDS

Aphids are major pest
our food plants and flo
Some aphid species ar
common on roses, whi
others spread diseases
which ruin potatoes ar
strawberries, as well as
many other food crops

*Intricate
pattern of
veins in wings*

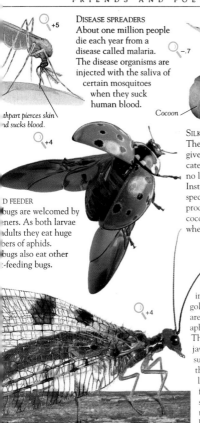

DISEASE SPREADERS
About one million people die each year from a disease called malaria. The disease organisms are injected with the saliva of certain mosquitoes when they suck human blood.

*thpart pierces skin
nd sucks blood.*

Moth

Cocoon

SILK PROVIDERS
The silk we use in clothes is given to us by silkworm moth caterpillars. Silkworm moths no longer occur in the wild. Instead, they are bred in special farms. The caterpillars produce the silk to form cocoons that protect them when they pupate.

D FEEDER
bugs are welcomed by
ners. As both larvae
dults they eat huge
bers of aphids.
bugs also eat other
-feeding bugs.

PEST EATERS
Lacewings are delicate insects, often with shining golden eyes. Their larvae are voracious predators of aphids and other plant lice. They have long, tubular jaws through which they suck the body contents of their prey. Lacewing larvae hide themselves from predators by sticking the remains of their prey onto small hairs on their back.

BEES AND POLLINATION

BEES AND PLANTS depend on each other.
Plants need bees to carry pollen
between flowers to produce seed.
Bees collect pollen and nectar
from flowers to feed their larvae.
Nectar in a hive is made into
honey for winter food.

BEE-KEEPING

For thousands of years people have
kept bees for their honey. Modern
hives have racks of frames, each with a
ready-made comb of cells. Individual frames
can be removed and the honey drained.

POLLINATION

Other insects, such as butterflies, also
pollinate flowers. Many flowers are a
special color or shape to attract
particular insects. These insects
receive pollen and nectar in
the process of carrying pollen
to another flower.

+2

+6

BASKETS
...arry pollen back to their nest in
... pollen baskets on their back legs.
...skets are made from curved
... A bee uses its front legs to
...ollen from its furry body and
...n the baskets.

Shape of dance shows bees direction of flowers.

BEE COMMUNICATION
When a honeybee finds
flowers with nectar it tells
other bees in the hive by
dancing. The bee conveys
the distance of the flowers
by how fast it shakes its
abdomen, and the
direction by the angle
of its dance.

Pollen
basket

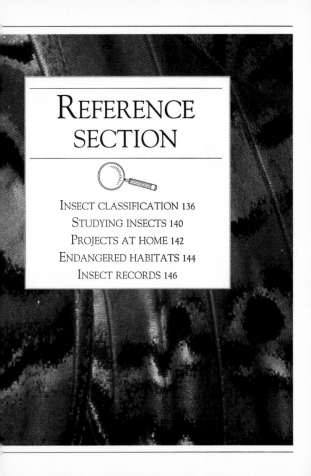

REFERENCE
SECTION

INSECT CLASSIFICATION 136
STUDYING INSECTS 140
PROJECTS AT HOME 142
ENDANGERED HABITATS 144
INSECT RECORDS 146

INSECT CLASSIFICATION

THE ONE million or so named insect species are par
the animal kingdom, which includes every other
animal species. In order to discuss the different spec
we classify them into a series of categories accordin
to the features they have in common. The largest
category is the kingdom, which includes all animal

The kingdom is divided i
smaller categories, which
are further divided until t
species level
is reached.

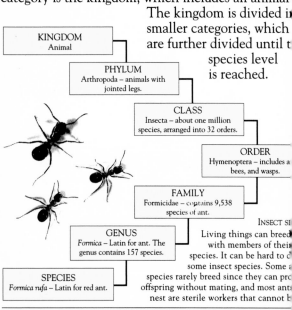

KINGDOM
Animal

PHYLUM
Arthropoda – animals with
jointed legs.

CLASS
Insecta – about one million
species, arranged into 32 orders.

ORDER
Hymenoptera – includes a
bees, and wasps.

FAMILY
Formicidae – contains 9,538
species of ant.

GENUS
Formica – Latin for ant. The
genus contains 157 species.

SPECIES
Formica rufa – Latin for red ant.

INSECT SI
Living things can breed
with members of their
species. It can be hard to c
some insect species. Some a
species rarely breed since they can pro
offspring without mating, and most ant
nest are sterile workers that cannot b

ORDER	SPECIES	CHARACTERISTICS
LEMBOLA	Springtails	Primitive wingless insects, often found on soil in vast numbers; incomplete metamorphosis
SANURA	Silverfish	Primitive wingless insects, found in caves and damp houses; incomplete metamorphosis
HEMEROPTERA	Mayflies	Larvae found in freshwater, adults have no feeding apparatus and live only a few days; incomplete metamorphosis
ONATA	Dragonflies and damselflies	Generally large insects found worldwide, either carnivorous or herbivorous, larvae are predators in freshwater; incomplete metamorphosis
COPTERA	Stone-flies	Adults are either herbivorous or do not feed at all and usually live along riverbanks, larvae live in freshwater; incomplete metamorphosis
TTODEA	Cockroaches	Omnivorous (eating both animals and plants) insects, often scavengers, found worldwide; incomplete metamorphosis
PTERA	Termites, also known as white ants	Social insects that live in vast colonies, each with one queen who lays all the eggs; most species feed on wood; incomplete metamorphosis
NTODEA	Mantids	Predatory insects with large eyes and grasping front legs, found mostly in the tropics; incomplete metamorphosis

ORDER	SPECIES	CHARACTERISTICS
DERMAPTERA	Earwigs	Omnivorous insects with fan-shaped hind wings and pincers on the abdom incomplete metamorphosis
ORTHOPTERA	Grasshoppers	Grass-feeding insects with jumping b legs; incomplete metamorphosis
PHASMATODEA	Leaf insects, stick insects	Leaf-feeding insects with camouflage flattened, or very slender bodies; incomplete metamorphosis
PSOCOPTERA	Book lice	Small chewing insects feeding on tre bark, in packs of food, and in book bindings – hence their name; incomplete metamorphosis
PHTHIRAPTERA	Parasitic lice	Parasites of birds and mammals, live skin and feed on feathers, skin, or blo wingless; incomplete metamorphosis
HEMIPTERA	Bugs	Insects with piercing and sucking mouthparts, feed on plants, insects, o mammals; incomplete metamorphosis
THYSANOPTERA	Thrips	Tiny insects with fringed wings, herbivorous with sucking mouthparts incomplete metamorphosis
MEGALOPTERA	Alderflies, dobson flies	Larvae are aquatic and carnivorous, adults have long antennae; incomple metamorphosis

ORDER	SPECIES	CHARACTERISTICS
NEUROPTERA	Lacewings, ant-lions	Predatory as larvae, adults are either carnivorous or herbivorous; incomplete metamorphosis
COLEOPTERA	Beetles	Very varied insects, with a hard front pair of wings covering the second pair, found worldwide; complete metamorphosis
MECOPTERA	Scorpion flies	Small predatory insects with biting mouthparts, found in woodlands, caterpillar-like larvae; complete metamorphosis
SIPHONAPTERA	Fleas	Wingless insects with jumping hind legs, parasites of birds and mammals, feeding on blood with piercing and sucking mouthparts; complete metamorphosis
DIPTERA	Flies	Adults feed on plants and animals and in rotting vegetation, found worldwide in all habitats, larvae (maggots) are legless; complete metamorphosis
TRICHOPTERA	Caddis flies	Larvae live in freshwater and build a protective case around their body, adults either feed from flowers or do not feed at all; complete metamorphosis
LEPIDOPTERA	Butterflies and moths	Larvae (caterpillars) feed mainly on plants but colorful adults drink nectar, adults of some species feed very little; complete metamorphosis
HYMENOPTERA	Wasps, ants, and bees	Mainly carnivorous insects although some are herbivorous, some species live in highly ordered societies; complete metamorphosis

STUDYING INSECTS

ONE OF THE BEST ways to learn about an insect is to study it up close, either by observing the insect in its natural habitat or by capturing a specimen for a short time to examine it even more closely. Keep a record of when and where the insect was found, and its appearance, behavior, and habitat.

Gall

OAK LEAF
WITH WASP
GALLS

MAKE AN INSECT TRAP

Even a small garden may contain hundreds of different types of insect. Setting up a series of pitfall traps is a good way of catching several insects for a closer look. You will need a trowel, plastic cups, large stones, and flat, square pieces of wood.

TROWEL

WOOD

STONES

CUPS

1 Dig a hole for a cup. The top of the cup must be at ground level. Put one cup inside another. You can remove the inner cup to examine your catch.

2 Put cups in different places around the garden: under trees, on bare soil, among herbs, next to a pond, or in the middle of the lawn.

3 Place the wood on stones over each trap to form a protective cover. Inspect the traps regularly and record which insects you find.

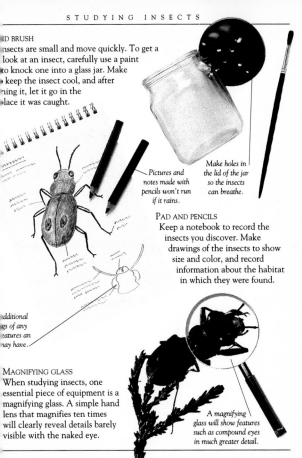

ND BRUSH
nsects are small and move quickly. To get a
look at an insect, carefully use a paint
o knock one into a glass jar. Make
keep the insect cool, and after
ning it, let it go in the
lace it was caught.

Pictures and notes made with pencils won't run if it rains.

Make holes in the lid of the jar so the insects can breathe.

PAD AND PENCILS
Keep a notebook to record the insects you discover. Make drawings of the insects to show size and color, and record information about the habitat in which they were found.

*dditional
gs of any
eatures an
nay have.*

MAGNIFYING GLASS
When studying insects, one essential piece of equipment is a magnifying glass. A simple hand lens that magnifies ten times will clearly reveal details barely visible with the naked eye.

A magnifying glass will show features such as compound eyes in much greater detail.

PROJECTS AT HOME

A CATERPILLAR
is an ideal
subject for
observing an
insect's life cycle. In
captivity, it will grow,
pupate, and finally emerge as
an adult. Keep a community of pond
insects in an aquarium to study the way
they live – both above and below the
surface of the water.

*Caterpilla
soft so they s
handled ge
Avoid har
caterpillars w
– these ma
and cause e*

CATERPILLAR BOX

When you have found a caterpillar, put it
in a box with plenty of leaves from its
feeding plant. Keep the box clean and dry
and replace the leaves as they are eaten
or begin to shrivel. After the caterpillar
pupates and becomes a butterfly or moth,
release it in the place the caterpillar was found.

INSECTS AND SAUCERS

Use three saucers of food
to see how different food
scents attract different
insects. Place fruit in
one saucer, gravy in
another, and water in the
third. Use white and yellow
saucers for the water, to see
if color draws insects.

*Butterflies and
wasps are drawn
to feed on the
sugary fruit.*

*The smell of the
meat in the
gravy will
attract insect
carnivores.*

*Clean water h
no smell – but
colored plate m
draw insects.*

TO MAKE YOUR OWN
T AQUARIUM

p an aquarium to observe
insects in a habitat like
own. You will need a
c aquarium, some gravel,
large stones, some dead
, and a few water plants.

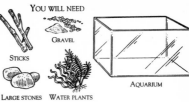

YOU WILL NEED

GRAVEL

STICKS

LARGE STONES   WATER PLANTS

AQUARIUM

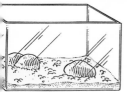

Cover the bottom of the
quarium with about 2 in (5 cm)
vel and scatter the large stones
d. The gravel will provide a
e for microscopic animals that
elp to keep the water clean.

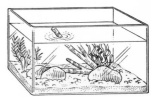

2 Fill the aquarium by pouring
water over an upside-down bowl.
In this way you do not disturb the
gravel. Next root the water plants
into the gravel and put in the sticks so
that they poke out above the water.

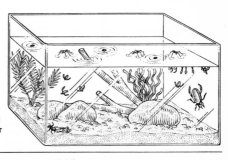

Using a pond net,
catch some insects
snails from a local
, place them in
aquarium, and
h what they do. You
can buy live
rfleas in a petshop.
help keep the
r clean and provide
d source of food for
redators.

143

ENDANGERED HABITATS

ALL OVER THE WORLD the natural environment is
shrinking as people exploit and destroy natural
habitats. The threats come from agriculture, forest,
mining, road building, the spread of towns, and
pollution. Even nature reserves can have problems
with increasing numbers of visitors. As habitats
disappear, so do the communities of plants, insects,
and other animals that live there.

HABITAT	REASONS FOR DESTRUCTION	INSECT EXAMPLE
RAINFOREST	Species-rich forests felled for timber or replaced by grasslands for cattle or crops. These support few insect species and are plagued by pests because the natural predators have gone.	Hercules beetle; Queen Alexandra birdwing butterfly; 8-spotted skipper butterfly; Wallace giant bee
FOREST	Large trees in forests felled for timber. Access roads in forest encourage farmers to settle who then clear more trees. Some trees and the insects associated with them threatened with extinction.	Periodical cicada; Giant carrion bee; Sugarfoot moth fly; European wood a; Frigate island gia; tenebrionid beetle
SEMIDESERT AREAS	Domestic livestock over-grazing leads to erosion of topsoil. Heat quickly evaporates irrigation water, resulting in salts building up in soil. Fewer plants can grow leading to expansion of deserts.	St. Helena earwig Belkin's dune tabanid fly; Avalo hairstreak butter; Ravoux's slavema; ant

HABITAT	REASONS FOR DESTRUCTION	INSECT EXAMPLES
...ICAL DRY ...T AREAS	Leaves fall off trees in dry season. Trees are destroyed by burning to produce grasslands for cattle. Fires are allowed to burn out of control. One of the most threatened habitats.	Giant wetas; Small hemiphlebia damselfly; Lord Howe Island stick insect; Australian nothomyrmecia ant
...RIES	Natural grasslands rich in wild flowers and insect species are plowed and treated with fertilizers and insecticides to produce cereal crops and "improved" grasslands for cattle.	Delta green ground beetle; Dakota skipper; Wiest's sphinx moth
...S AND RIVERS	Water is polluted by fertilizers running off fields. Pollution from sewage and industrial waste, and metal pollution from mine wastes. River channels are straightened and dredged.	Large blue lake mayfly; Freya's damselfly; Relict Himalayan dragonfly; Florida spiketail dragonfly; Tobias caddis fly
...SSLANDS	Drainage of water meadows and plowing of grasslands for crops destroys natural plants. Addition of fertilizers results in domination by aggressive species of grass with fewer wild flowers and insects.	Pygmy hog sucking louse; Large blue butterfly; Bay checkerspot butterfly
...S AND ...LANDS	Land is drained for agriculture, such as planting of timber trees for commercial forestry. Cutting and extraction of peat for use in gardens or as fuel for power stations.	Ohio emerald dragonfly; Flumiense swallowtail butterfly; Harris' mimic swallowtail butterfly

INSECT RECORDS

INSECTS ARE the most numerous animals on Ear
Their success is mostly due to their small size a
remarkable adaptability. The following are som
of the more amazing insect record-breakers.

SIZE

- Bulkiest insect: goliath beetle – 4⅓ in (110 mm) long weighing 3½ oz (100 g)
- Smallest: mymarid wasp – 0.0067 in (17 mm) long
- Largest wingspan: *Thysania agrippina* moth – 11 in (28 cm) wide
- Largest water insect: giant water bug from Venezuela and Brazil – 4½ in (11.5 cm) long
- Most numerous insect: springtails – about 540,000 per sq ft (50,000 per sq m) in grassland

FLIGHT

- Fastest ever: a giant prehistoric dragonfly probably had to fly at least 43 mph (69 km/h) to stay airborne
- Fastest-flying living insects: hawk-moths – reach top speed of 33⅓ mph (53.6 km/h)
- Fastest wingbeat: the midge *Forcipomyia* – 62,760 beats per minute
- Slowest wingbeat: swallowtail butterfly – 300 beats per minute
- Farthest migration: painted lady butterfly – 4,000 miles (6,436 km) from North Africa to Iceland

PESTS

- Most fatalities: m than half of all dea since the Stone A are due to malaria carrying mosquito Rat fleas carry a pla which killed 20 million people in 14th-century Euro
- Most poisonous: about 40,000 peop are killed each year wasp or bee sting
- Most disease-ridd the housefly transm more than 30 disea and parasites
- Most destructive locust swarm can e 20,000 tons (tonne of crops per day

NESTS

• Largest: Australian termite nests – up to 23 ft (7 m) high and 100 ft (31 m) in diameter at the base

• Tallest: nests of African termite – 42 ft (12.8 m) high

• Deepest: nests of desert termite – 131 ft (40 m) below ground

COMMUNICATION

• Loudest: cicada – song can be heard by humans from a distance of ¼ mile (400 m).

• Most sensitive sense of smell: Indian moon moth – can detect pheromones of a mate from a distance of over 6¾ miles (11 km)

LEGS/ANTENNAE

• Longest: giant stick insect – 20 in (51 cm)

• Longest antennae: New guinea longhorn beetle – 7½ in (20 cm)

• Longest jump: Desert locust – 19½ in (50 cm), which is 10 times its own body length

TOUGHEST

• Larvae of ephyrid flies live in the waters of hot springs at 140° F (60°C)

• The snow flea remains active at temperatures of 5° F (-15°C)

• Larvae of the midge *Polypedilum* can survive years without water and three days in liquid nitrogen (-321°F, -196°C)

LIFESTYLE

• Longest lifecycle: periodic cicada – 17 years

• Longest-lived larva: a wood-boring beetle larva once survived for 45 years

• Shortest-lived insect: fruitfly – can complete its entire lifecycle in less than 14 days

EGGS

• Largest: ⅜ in x ¹⁄₂₀ in (10.2 mm x 4.2 mm) laid by cerambycid beetle, *Titanus giganteus*

• Longest time in the egg stage: 9½ months by the cerambycid beetle *Saperda carcharia*

• Most eggs laid: the queen *Macrotermes* termite can lay 40,000 eggs per day

Resources

USEFUL ADDRESSES:

UNITED STATES

PLACES WITH INSECT
COLLECTIONS TO VISIT:

**American Museum of
Natural History**
Central Park West at
79th Street
New York, NY 10024

**Buffalo Museum of
Science**
1020 Humboldt
Parkway,
Buffalo, NY 14211

Butterfly World
3600 West Sample
Road
Coconut Creek,
FL 33073

**The Carnegie Museum
of Natural History**
4400 Forbes Avenue
Pittsburgh, PA 15213

**The Denver Museum
of Natural History**
2001 Colorado Blvd.
Denver, CO 80205

The Field Museum
1200 South Lakeshore
Drive Chicago,
IL 60605

**Houston Museum of
Natural Science**
1 Hermann Circle
Drive
Houston, TX 77030

Liberty Science Center
251 Philip Street
Jersey City, NJ 07305

**Natural History
Museum of Los
Angeles County**
900 Exposition Blvd.
Los Angeles,
CA 90007

The National Mus
of Natural History
Smithsonian
Institution
Dept. of Entomolo
Attn: Collections N
Mail Stop #: NHB
Constitution Ave.
10th Street, N.W.
Washington,
D.C. 20560

The Schiele Muse
of Natural History
Planetarium, INC.
1500 East Garrison
Blvd.
Gastonia, NC 280

SOCIETIES TO JOIN:

Entomological Soc
of Maryland
9301 Annapolis Rc
Lanham, MD 207(

The Lepidopterists
Society
c/o Allen Press
P.O. Box 368
Lawrence, KS 660

achusetts
rfly Society
Cocasset Street
rough,
02035

York
nological Society
merican Museum
ural History
al Park West at
Street
York, NY 10024

n American
rfly Association
aware Road
stown, NJ 07960

oung
nologists' Society
Peggy Place
g, MI 48910

CANADA

Biological Survey of Canada
(Terrestrial Arthropods)
Canadian Museum
of Nature
P.O. Box 3443
Station D, Ottawa,
Ontario, RIP 6P4

British Columbia Museum
675 Bellville Street
Victoria, British
Columbia, V6T 1W5

Manitoba Museum of Man and Nature
Winnipeg
Manitoba, 43B 0N2

Nova Scotia Museum
1747 Summer Street
Halifax, Nova Scotia,
H3H 3A6

Royal Ontario Museum
Dept. of Entomology
100 Queens Park
Toronto, Ontario,
M5S 2C6

Toronto Entomologists Association
c/o 34 Seaton Drive
Aurora, Ontario,
L4G 2K1

University of British Columbia
Spencer Entomological
Museum
Dept. of Zoology
Vancouver, British
Columbia, V6T 1W5

SOCIETIES TO JOIN:

Entomological Society of Canada
393 Winston Avenue
Ottawa, Ontario,
K2A 1Y8

Entomological Society of Quebec
M.C. Bouchard,
Complexe Scientifique,
D-1-59,
2700 rue Einstein,
Ste-Foy, Quebec

Glossary

ABDOMEN
Segmented section of arthropod's body behind thorax which contains the digestive and reproductive organs.

ANTENNAE
Two appendages on the head of insects and other arthropods used mainly for touching and smelling.

ARTHROPOD
An invertebrate with jointed appendages and a hardened exoskeleton.

BROOD CELL
A space or structure in a bee or wasp nest where a single egg is laid and the larva develops until it becomes an adult.

CAMOUFLAGE
The means of disguising the body in order to go unnoticed by predators or prey.

CARNIVOROUS
Flesh-eating.

CASTE
In social insect societies, a group containing individuals which

perform specialized tasks, such as "workers" in wasp nests or "soldiers" in ant nests.

CATERPILLAR
Any wormlike insect larva, but usually refers to the larva of moths and butterflies.

CERCI
Two spine-shaped sensory growths at the end of the abdomen of some arthropods.

CHRYSALIS
The pupa of a moth or butterfly.

CLASPERS
Two pincerlike appendages on the abdomen of male insects which grasp the female during mating.

COCOON
Protective silk casing which the larvae of many insects weave around themselves prior to pupation.

COLONY
A group of social insects living and working together and sharing a nest.

COMPLETE METAMORPHOSIS
The type of development from egg to adult in which there are distinct stages including a pupal stage, usually the larva looks very different from the adult and also has a different diet.

COMPOUND EYE
An eye composed of many separate eyes called ommatidia. Each ommatidium is capable of vision.

COURTSHIP DANCE
Dancelike movement, often performed in flight, between two insects before mating.

DISRUPTIVE COLORATION
A combination of colors and patterns on the body which disrupt its shape, making it hard to recognize.

ELYTRA
The front wings of beetles which are hardened and protect the body.

TOMOLOGY
scientific study of
cts.

SKELETON
external skeleton of
rthropod.

SPOTS
rkings on an insect's
y which look like
s for frightening or
racting predators.

SIL
remains of
ething that once
d, preserved as stone.

NGUS
imple plant, usually
wing on other plants
animals and often
sing decay and
ase.

NGUS GARDEN
gus cultivated in a
t as food by leaf-
ter ants and certain
cies of termite.

LL
abnormal growth on
ant caused by the
sence of an insect's
or its feeding
vities.

LS
growths on an
atic insect's body by
ch the insect
athes underwater.

GRUB
An insect larva,
especially of beetles,
which lives underground
or in rotting wood.

HALTERES
The hind wings of flies
(Diptera) which have
been modified into
clubbed stalks and are
used as balancers
in flight.

HERBIVOROUS
Plant-eating.

HONEYDEW
A sweet, sticky liquid
secreted by aphids and
treehoppers, derived
from the sap of plants on
which they feed.

HONEY GUIDES
Lines on the flower
petals of certain plants
which reflect ultraviolet
light and direct
insects to the pollen
and nectar.

HOST
Animal or plant on
which a parasite or
herbivore feeds and
lays its eggs.

**INCOMPLETE
METAMORPHOSIS**
The type of
development of insects
in which the nymphs

hatch looking like small
versions of the adults
and there is no
pupal stage.

INVERTEBRATE
An animal without a
backbone.

LARVA
The stage in an insect's
life between egg and
pupa. The young stage
of insects that do
not pupate is called
a nymph.

LEAF MINERS
Insects which live and
feed inside a leaf,
creating a mine, or
tunnel, as they feed.

MAMMAL
A warm-blooded animal
which drinks its
mother's milk when it
is young.

MATING
The reproductive act
between a male and
female of the same
species where the male
puts sperm in the female
in order to create young.

METAMORPHOSIS
The process of insect
growth from egg to adult
by which the body shape
metamorphoses, or
changes, as it grows.

MIMICRY
The process whereby
one insect species copies
the coloration and
behavior of another
species, usually for the
purpose of protection
from predators.

MOLTING
The shedding of old
skin to be replaced by
a new skin.

MUD PUDDLING
The habit of butterflies,
usually in the tropics,
of gathering in groups
to drink from muddy
puddles in order to
obtain essential
minerals and salts.

NECTAR
A sugary fluid found
in flowers.

NOCTURNAL
Being active by night
and resting by day.

NYMPH
See LARVA.

OCELLI
Simple eyes which have
a limited function,
probably only detecting
light and shade.

OMMATIDIUM
A single part of a
compound eye capable
of detailed vision.

OMNIVOROUS
Having a diet of both
animal and plant food.

OVIPOSITOR
The egg-laying tube of
insects.

PARASITE
An animal which
completes its
development on, or in,
the body of another
animal without
benefiting its host in
any way.

PALPS
Sensory organs beside
the jaws of some insects.

PHEROMONES
Chemicals produced by
insects of both sexes
which act as a sexual
attractant to members
of the opposite sex.

POLLEN
A flower's male sex cells
which fertilize the
female sex cell (ovule).

POLLINATION
The process by which
the pollen of one
flower is transported,
usually by insects or
by the wind, to the
female part (ovary) of
another plant of the
same species to
produce seeds.

PREDATOR
An animal which hu
other animals for foo

PROLEGS
Also known as false l
fleshy growths on the
abdomen of some ins
larvae, especially
caterpillars, which
function as legs.

PUPA, PUPAL STAGE
The inactive, non-
feeding stage of insec
which undergo comp
metamorphosis, whe
the larva transforms
an adult.

ROSTRUM
The piercing and
sucking, beaklike
mouthparts of true b

SALIVA
A liquid secreted int
the mouth which beg
the process of digestin
food. In some insects
saliva is deadly and is
injected into prey,
killing the prey and
dissolving its insides.

SCALES
Modified hairs which
have become flattene
especially found in
butterflies and moths

SIMPLE EYE
See OCELLI.

CIAL
ving in groups.

LDIER
caste member from a
mite or ant colony
ich has an enlarged
ad and jaws used in a
fensive role to protect
e other nest members.

ECIES
group of animals or
ants which can breed
ly with each other
d produce fertile
spring.

ERM
male cell which is put
side a female during
ating to join with her
gcell, which creates a
w individual.

IRACLES
ternal openings of the
cheae on the body of
insect through which
e insect breathes.

ITTLE
othy liquid produced
certain plant bugs
which they hide
m predators and
ich stops them
m dehydrating.

ING
he modified ovipositor
certain wasps, bees,
d ants, which has
lost its egg-laying
function and is used to
inject venom into prey
or enemies.

STYLET
A piercing needlelike
organ, usually a
mouthpart of bugs and
certain blood-sucking
insects.

SWARMING
Any huge group of
insects traveling
together, but usually the
behavior of honeybees
when the queen and a
large number of workers
leave their nest to set up
a new nest elsewhere.

TARSUS
The insect's "foot,"
consisting of between
one and five segments
and one or two claws for
gripping surfaces.

TEMPERATE REGIONS
Parts of the Earth
between the tropical
and the polar regions,
with moderate
temperatures.

THORAX
The part of an
arthropod's body
between the head and
abdomen that bears
the legs and wings.

TRACHEAE
Tubes in the body
of an insect which
transport oxygen.

TROPICAL REGIONS
Parts of the Earth
around the equator
with hot temperatures
all year.

ULTRAVIOLET
Beyond the violet end
of the light spectrum,
ultraviolet is invisible
to most mammals, but
visible to most insects.

VENOM
A poison which is often
deadly, produced by
many predatory insects
for injecting into prey
or enemies.

WARNING COLORATION
Bright, conspicuous
body coloring used by
many insects with
weapons or poisonous
bodies; predators learn
to avoid these insects.

WORKER
A member of an
insect colony which is
sterile (cannot breed)
and whose duties
include caring for the
larvae, maintaining
the nest, and foraging
for food.

Latin name index

African cave cricket (*Pholeogryllus geertsi*)

African driver ant (*Dorylus nigricans*)

African goliath beetle (*Goliathus cacicus*)

Basker moth (*Euchromia lethe*)

Bedbug (*Cimex lectularius*)

Bumblebee (*Bombus terrestris*)

Cardinal beetle (*Pyrochroa coccinea*)

Carpet beetle (*Anthrenus verbasci*)

Cinnabar moth (*Tyria jacobeae*)

Cockchafer beetle (*Melolontha melolontha*)

Colorado beetle (*Leptinotarsa decimlineata*)

Comma butterfly (*Polygonia c-album*)

Common darter dragonfly (*Sympetrum striolatum*)

Common earwig (*Forficula auricularia*)

Common field grasshopper (*Chorthippus brunneus*)

Common mormon butterfly (*Papilio polytes*)

Common wasp (*Vespula vulgaris*)

Common yellow dung fly (*Scathophaga stercoraria*)

Crane-fly (*Tipula maxima*)

Darwin's beetle (*Chiasognathus granti*)

Death-watch beetle (*Xestobium rufovillosum*)

Desert locust (*Schistocerca gregaria*)

Desert-dwelling cricket (*Schizodactylus monstrosus*)

Devil's coach horse beetle (*Staphylinus olens*)

Elm bark beetle (*Scolytus scolytus*)

English swallowtail butterfly (*Papilio machaon*)

Flour beetle (*Tenebrio molitor*)

Froghopper (*Philaenus spumarius*)

Furniture beetle (*Anobium punctatum*)

Giant lacewing (*Osmylu fulvicephalus*)

Giant wood wasp (*Uroc gigas*)

Grayling butterfly (*Hipparchia semele*)

Great diving beetle (*Dy marginalis*)

Green hairstreak butter (*Callophrys rubi*)

Green oak tortrix moth (*Tortrix viridana*)

Green weaver ant (*Oecophylla smaragdina*)

Hawker dragonfly (*Aesh cyanea*)

Helicopter damselfly (*Megaloprepus caerulatus*)

Hornet moth (*Sesia apiformis*)

Housefly (*Musca domest*)

Human flea (*Pulex irrita*)

Indian leaf butterfly (*K inachus*)

Jewel wasp (*Ampulex compressa*)

Jeweled frog beetle (*Sag buqueti*)

ern bug (*Fulgora*
...aria*)

...e blue butterfly
...culinea arion*)

...e copper butterfly
...aena dispar*)

...e white (cabbage white)
...erfly (*Pieris brassicae*)

...eay's spectre
...atosoma tiaratum*)

...ble gall wasp (*Andricus
...ri*)

...bled white
...erfly (*Melanargia
...hea*)

...veille du jour moth
...hmonia aprilina*)

...ican bean beetle
...achna varivestis*)

...e cricket (*Gryllotalpa
...otalpa*)

...arch butterfly (*Danaus
...ppus*)

...hib Desert beetle
...ymacris unguicularis*)

...weevil (*Curculio
...lium*)

...bush cricket (*Meconema
...ssinum*)

Oak silkmoth
(*Antheraea harti*)

Parent bug (*Elasmucha grisea*)

Parasol ant (*Atta cephalotes*)

Peacock butterfly (*Inachis io*)

Pond skater (*Gerris gibbifer*)

Postman butterfly (*Heliconius
melpomene*)

Purple emperor (*Apatura iris*)

Puss moth (*Cerura vinula*)

Saddle-back moth (*Sibine
stimulea*)

Silver-spotted skipper
butterfly (*Epargyreus clarus*)

Silver-striped hawk-moth
(*Hippotion celerio*)

Silver-washed fratillary
butterfly (*Argynnis paphia*)

Small postman butterfly
(*Heliconius erato*)

Snakefly (*Raphidia notata*)

Soldier beetle (*Rhagonycha
fulva*)

South American dung beetle
(*Coprophanaeus lancifer*)

Speckled bush cricket
(*Leptophyes punctatissima*)

Speckled wood butterfly
(*Pararge aegeria*)

Springtail (*Isotoma palustris*)

Spurge hawk-moth (*Hyles
euphorbiae*)

Stag beetle (*Lucanus cervus*)

Stonefly (*Diura bipunctata*)

Striped blue crow butterfly
(*Euploea mulciber*)

Striped-winged grasshopper
(*Stenobothrus lineatus*)

Surinam cockroach
(*Pycnoscelis surinamensis*)

Tarantula hawk wasp (*Pepsis
heros*)

Tiger beetle (*Cicindela
campestris*)

Vapourer moth (*Orgyia
antiqua*)

Water boatman (*Notonecta
glauca*)

Water measurer (*Hydrometra
stagnorum*)

Water scorpion (*Nepa
cinerea*)

Weevil-hunting wasp
(*Cerceris arenaria*)

West African termites
(*Macrotermes bellicosus*)

Whirligig beetle (*Dineutes
politus*)

Wood ant (*Formica rufa*)

Wood cricket
(*Nemobius sylvestris*)

Index

A

abdomen, 13
acid, ants, 17, 34
acorns, 67
African crickets, 118
alderflies, 138
alligator mimics, 58
amber, resin, 14
anatomy, 12-3
antennae, 18, 34-5, 102, 147
ant-lions, 83, 139
ants, 16-7, 34, 37, 53, 139
  anteaters, 81
  habitats, 110-1, 117
  nests, 48, 74, 98
aphids, 48, 128, 130-1
  reproduction, 44, 136
aquariums, 143
arthropods, 13
assassin bugs, 20, 39, 56
atlas moths, 106

B

bark insects, 72
basker moths, 56
bees, 16-7, 48, 139, 146
  pollination, 132-3
beetles, 16, 29, 34, 37, 139
  flight, 30-1
  habitats, 75, 80-1, 83, 90,
  96-7, 104-5
  hunting, 52, 53
  metamorphosis, 44
  pests, 126-7
  soil-dwellers, 120-1
birds, 94

birdwing butterflies, 101
bogs, 145
Borneo, 15, 96
breathing, 12
breeding, 40-3, 136
bugs, 20, 127, 138
bulldog ants, 37
bumblebees, 48, 65
burrowing insects, 82
butterflies, 18, 29, 124-5, 139
  camouflage, 55
  courtship flights, 40
  eggs, 43
  habitats, 70-1, 74, 81-2, 94,
  100-3, 129
  hibernation, 119
  metamorphosis, 24-5
  proboscis, 38-9
  see also caterpillars

C

cabbage white butterflies, 124
cacti, 115
caddis flies, 86-7, 90, 139
camouflage, 54-5, 94-5
carnivores, 52, 90
carpet beetles, 127
caterpillars, 13, 18, 32, 56, 97
  "false legs," 27
  feeding, 36
  as food, 49
  metamorphosis, 24-5
  moths, 65, 66, 129
  parasites, 53
  studying, 142
  survival techniques, 46-7

caves, 61, 114-5, 118-9
cerambycid beetles, 147
cerci, 13
chafer beetles, 46
chalcid wasps, 67
chrysalises, 25
cicadas, 96, 121, 147
cinnabar moths, 79
click beetles, 121
cockchafer beetles, 30-1
cockroaches, 21, 125, 13
  as food, 53, 117
  habitats, 114, 119
  colonies, 48-51, 98-9
Colorado beetles, 124
colour, 18, 32, 33, 95, 14
  camouflage, 54-5
  mimicry, 58-9
  warning colouration, 5
comma butterflies, 71
communication, 34, 133
conifer forests, 65
copal, 14
courtship, 40-1
crane-flies, 19, 29
crickets, 34, 95, 121
  habitats, 74, 80, 83, 11
  oak bush crickets, 68-9

D

damselflies, 41, 107, 137
  metamorphosis, 22-3
darkling beetles, 115
Darwin, Charles, 104
Darwin's beetles, 104
Darwin's hawk-moths, 3

watch beetles, 126
, 61, 114-5, 116-7
coach horses, 121, 128
s, insect-spread, 131
 flies, 138
flies, 21, 28, 91, 137
32
ng, 36
ats, 86
storic, 15, 146
ng, 38-9
ants, 110-1
eetles, 43, 80, 105
ies, 19, 82

4-5
, 14, 43, 138
y, 130
2, 24, 40-4, 147
nflies, 91
irds, 44
es, 45
rk beetles, 73
flies, 41
gered habitats, 144-5
d flies, 147
tes, 94
on, 14-5
leton, 12, 13
2-3
ts, on wings, 29, 57

g, 20, 36-7, 42-3, 67
hafers, 78
rickets, 83
sects, 14-5
0, 139, 146

flies, 18-9, 28-9, 127, 139
flight, 26, 30-1, 40, 146
flour beetles, 13, 126
flowers, 14, 33, 59, 65, 132-3
forests, tropical, 61, 92-111,
    144-5
fossils, 14-5
freshwater habitats, 61, 84-91
fritillaries, 70
frog beetles, 97
froghoppers, 44-5
fungus, 51, 111

G
galls, 67
garden insects, 61, 128-9
geometrid moths, 59, 68
giant water bugs, 146
glowworms, 40
goliath beetles, 107, 146
grasshoppers, 21, 30, 129, 138
    stripe-winged, 54
    warning colouration, 57
grasslands, 60, 76-81, 145
grayling butterflies, 82
great diving beetles, 16, 90-1
green hairstreaks, 70
green oak tortrix moths, 66
greenhouses, 125
ground beetles, 37, 52, 75
growth, 22-5, 44-5
grubs see larvae

H
hairs, sensory, 34
halteres, 28, 29
harvester ants, 37
hawk-moths, 38, 129, 146
heads, 13

hearing, 34-5
hearts, 12
heathlands, 60, 76-9, 82-3
helicopter damselflies, 107
hercules moths, 146
hibernation, 119
hives, 132
honey, 48, 132
honey guides, 33
honeybees, 17
honeydew, 48
honeypot ants, 117
horned beetles, 104-5
hornet mimics, 58
horseflies, 39
houseflies, 19, 27, 39, 127
    records, 146-7
household insects, 126-7
hoverflies, 19, 31, 128
hunting, 52-3

I
ichneumon wasps, 17, 42
inchworms, 59, 68
Indian leaf butterflies, 55
iridescence, 18

J
jaws, 36-7, 52
jewel wasps, 53, 117
jumping, 26-7

L
lacewings, 28, 131, 139
ladybirds, 44, 131
lakes, 61, 84-91, 145
lamellicorn beetles, 120
large blue butterflies, 81
large copper butterflies, 79

larvae, 12, 24, 26, 42-3, 53
  caddis flies, 86-7, 90
  ladybirds, 44
  "leather-jackets", 19
  mosquitoes, 89
  soil-dwellers, 120-1
  survival techniques, 46-7
  wasps, 49, 99
  see also caterpillars; maggots; nymphs
leaf insects, 108-9, 138
leaf litter, 121
legs, 26-7, 147
lenses, compound eyes, 33
lice, 126, 138
lichen, 73
locusts, 21, 30, 45, 116, 146-7
  jumping, 26-7, 147
longhorn beetles, 35, 147

M

Macleay's spectre, 108
Macrotermes termites, 147
maggots, 13, 19, 127
Malay lacewing butterflies, 43
mandibles, bugs, 20
mantids, 21, 41, 47, 55, 137
marbled white butterflies, 81
mayflies, 45, 90, 137
mealworms, 126
merveille du jour moths, 73
metamorphosis, 22-5, 44-5
Mexican bean beetles, 46
migration, 146
mimicry, 58-9, 103, 108-9
mole crickets, 121
monarch butterflies, 125
moon moths, 147
mormon butterflies, 47

morpho butterflies, 100
mosquitoes, 89, 131, 146
mosquitoes, 89, 131, 146
moths, 18, 29, 100, 106, 139
  caterpillars, 66
  coloration, 54, 56-7
  mimicry, 58-9
  proboscis, 38-9
  senses, 35
mouthparts, 36, 38-9
movement, 26-7, 30
muscles, 26-7, 30
mymarid wasps, 146

N

Namib Desert beetles, 115, 116
nectar, 14, 38, 132
Nero butterflies, 100
nerve cord, 12
nests, 48-51, 98-9, 147
nymphs:
  damselflies, 22-3
  dragonflies, 21, 91
  earwigs, 43
  froghoppers, 44-5
  locusts, 21, 45, 116
  mantids, 21
  mayflies, 45, 90

O

ocelli, 33
ommatidia, 33
orchids, 94
ovipositors, 42
Oxford ragwort, 79

P

painted lady butterflies, 146
palps, 36

parasites, 42, 53, 126,
parasol ants, 110-1
peacock butterflies, 11
peatlands, 145
pests, 60, 124-7, 146
pheromones, 40, 147
pink-winged stick inse
pitfall traps, 140
poisonous insects, 103
  warning coloration, 5
pollen, 14, 81, 132-3
pollination, 132-3
polyphemus moths, 18
pond skaters, 89
ponds, 86-91, 143
postman butterflies, 9
103
prairies, 145
praying mantises, 37
predators, 52-3, 56-7, 5
  hiding from, 54-5, 58
proboscis, 38-9
processionary moths, 6
pupas, 24-5, 44, 142
purple emperors, 69
purple hairstreaks, 70
puss moth caterpillars,

Q

queens, 48
  ants, 110
  termites, 50, 51

R

ragwort, 79, 81
rainforests *see* tropical
red admirals, 129
reproduction, 40-3, 13
rhinoceros beetles, 104

, 61, 84-91, 145
ms, 39
eetles, 53

-back caterpillars, 56
la carcharia, 147
ze flies, 110
, wings, 29
34-5, 40, 102
on flies, 139
esert areas, 144
bugs, 20, 30, 45
oths, 57, 102, 131
spotted skippers, 129
-washed fritillary, 70
fish, 137
06-7, 146
, ants, 110
ng, 34-5
lies, 72
fleas, 147
insects, 48-51, 98-9
sects, 61, 114-5, 120-1
r insects, 50, 81, 111
ed bush crickets, 80
led woods, 71
wasps, 107
les, 120
tails, 53, 137, 146
cats, 78, 87
e hawk moths, 120
flies, 38
eetles, 16, 75, 105
nsects, 21, 147, 138
uflage, 108-9
wasps, 17
ugs, 45
lies, 47, 137

striped blue crow butterflies,
   102
stylets, 39
swallowtail butterflies, 18, 25
   41, 64, 146
sweat bees, 14
swimming, 26

T

tarantula hawk wasps, 17
tarantulas, 107
tarsus, 13
termites, 48, 50-1, 137, 147
thorax, 13
thrips, 138
tiger beetles, 83, 114
Titanus giganteus, 147
town habitats, 61, 122-33
trachea, 12
traps, 140-1
tree ants, 48
treehoppers, 54, 58-9
trees, 64
   canopies, 68-9, 96-9
   oaks, 64, 66-9
   temperate woodlands, 60,
   62-75
   tropical forests, 61, 92-111,
   144-5
   trunks and branches, 72-3

U

ultraviolet light, 33
underwater insects, 90-1

V

vaporer moths, 65
violet ground beetles, 75
violin beetles, 97

W

wasps, 16-7, 29, 69, 107, 139
   habitats, 117, 125
   eggs, 43
   eyes, 33
   hunting, 43, 52
   mimicking, 58
   nests, 48-9, 98-9
   parasitic, 42, 53
   stings, 146
water boatmen, 26, 88-9
water measurers, 89
water scorpions, 87
waterfleas, 143
wax, 48
weaver ants, 98
weevil-hunting wasps, 43, 52
weevils, 67
wetlands, 64, 145
whirligig beetles, 88
white admirals, 75
wings, 18, 20, 28-9, 30-1, 57
   beetles, 13, 16, 29
   butterflies and moths, 18,
   25, 29
   cockroaches, 21
   damselflies, 23
   dragonflies, 21, 28
   shield bugs, 20
wireworms, 121
wood ants, 17, 74
wood-boring beetles, 147
wood crickets, 74
wood wasps, 72
woolly bears, 127
workers, 49, 50, 51

Y

yellow dung flies, 19, 82

Acknowledgments

Dorling Kindersley would like to thank:
Laura Buller for editorial supervision, Robert Graham for additional research and editorial support, Sarah Cowley for final text fitting, and Hilary Bird for compiling the index.

Photographs by:
Julie Anderson; Jane Burton; Peter Chadwick; Neil Fletcher; Frank Greenaway; Colin Keates; Dave King; Andrew McRobb; Oxford Scientific Films; Tim Ridley; Bill Sands; Kim Taylor; Jerry Young.

Illustrations by:
John Davis; Ted Dewan; Nick Hall; Brian Hargreaves; Nick Hewetson; John Hutchison; Mark Iley; Richard Lewington; Ruth Lindsay; Tommy Swahn; Simon Thomas; John Woodcock; Colin Woolf.

Picture credits: t = top b = bottom c = center l = left r = right
Bruce Coleman/Eric Crichton 60cl, 62-63; Gerald Cubitt 61br, 92-93; Geoff Doré 61bc, 84-85; P.A. Hinchcliffe 40tr; Eckart Pott 125tc; Dr Sandro Prato 131tr; Hans Reinhard 83tl; Kevin Rushby 43tl; Dr Frieder Sauer 59br; Kim Taylor 31tr, 70cr, 78cr, 125tl;
Norman Tomalin 94c. Natural Hi Museum/Frank Greenaway 82cr; Natural Science Photos/M. Boular 121bc; P. Bowman 74cl; M. Chine 127cl; Carol Farneti 94bl; Adrian Hoskins 79cr; Richard Revels 74tr 124cr; P.H. & S.L. Ward 41cr, 129 David Yendall 87tr. Oxford Scien Films/Kathie Atkinson 37tr; G.I. Bernard 87cl; Raymond Blythe 12(Densey Clyne 117tr; C.M. Collins J.A.L. Cooke 59c, 126tl; Michael Fogden 115tl; Peter Gathercole 47 Mantis Wildlife Films 12cl; Peter O'Toole 48cr; James Robinson 56c 83br; Harold Taylor 65c; Steve T 61cr, 112-113, 115tr; P. & W. Wa 114cr. Premaphotos/K.G. Preston-Mafham 39tr, 47br, 51br, 53cl, 54 60br, 76-77, 94br, 98bl, 111t, 111c Dr. Bill Sands 50cr. Science Phot Library/J.C. Revy 102cr. Tony Sto Images/Mike Surowiak 87bc.

Every effort has been made to trace the copyright holders and we apologize in advance for any unintentional omissions. We wou be pleased to insert the appropriate acknowledgment in any subsequen edition of this publication.